A FIELD GUIDE TO
U.S. CONGREGATIONS

A FIELD GUIDE TO U.S. CONGREGATIONS

Who's Going Where and Why

Cynthia Woolever and Deborah Bruce

Westminster John Knox Press
LOUISVILLE • LONDON

U.S. CONGREGATIONS

The U.S. Congregational Life Survey was conducted in compliance with the American Association for Public Opinion Research's (AAPOR) Code of Professional Ethics and Practices, which may be found on the AAPOR Web site at www.aapor.org/ethics.

Book design by PerfecType, Nashville, Tennessee
Cartoons: © Chris Morgan, *cjmorgan@ozemail.com.au, first published in* Winds of Change, *1994 and* Shaping a Future, *1997.*
Cover design by Mark Abrams
Cover photographs: Courtesy of Corbis and Comstock

First edition
Published by Westminster John Knox Press
Louisville, Kentucky

This book is printed on acid-free paper that meets the American National Standards Institute Z39.48 standard. ♾

PRINTED IN THE UNITED STATES OF AMERICA

02 03 04 05 06 07 08 09 10 11 — 10 9 8 7 6 5 4 3 2 1

Library of Congress Cataloging-in-Publication data is on file at the Library of Congress, Washington, D.C.

ISBN 0-664-22569-1

CONTENTS

PREFACE

The International Congregational Life Survey (ICLS) was initiated in 1999 as a collaborative effort of four countries. Extending the National Church Life Survey (NCLS) used earlier in Australia, the aim is to provide mission resources for congregations and parishes based on results from a survey of worshipers in four nations. The ICLS project was conducted in April and May 2001, with more than 12,000 congregations and 1.2 million worshipers participating. Each congregation invited all worshipers to complete a survey. The congregations also completed a congregational profile form, and the key leader in each congregation answered questions as well. Survey results are being used to provide individualized reports to each participating congregation and to produce books, research reports, and other resources about religious life in the twenty-first century.

The ICLS is conducted by the following agencies and people:

Australia: National Church Life Survey (NCLS) sponsored by ANGLICARE NSW of the Anglican Church in Australia, the New South Wales Board of Mission of the Uniting Church in Australia, and the Australian Catholic Bishops Conference: Dean Drayton (convener of the ICLS steering committee), John Bellamy, Howard Dillon*, Robert Dixon, Peter Kaldor (founding director of NCLS and international coordinator), Ruth Powell, and Tina Rendell*

England: Churches Information for Mission (CIM): Phillip Escott, Alison Gelder*, Roger Whitehead*

New Zealand: Church Life Survey–New Zealand (CLS–NZ) is a subcommittee of the Christian Research Association of New Zealand: Norman Brookes*

United States: U.S. Congregations supported by Lilly Endowment Inc., the Louisville Institute, and the Research Services office of the Presbyterian Church (U.S.A.): Deborah Bruce, Cynthia Woolever*, Keith Wulff*. The key leader survey, completed by the pastor, priest, minister, rabbi, or other leader, was conducted in partnership with the Pulpit & Pew project, based at Duke University Divinity School, and funded by Lilly Endowment Inc.

* ICLS Steering Committee

ACKNOWLEDGMENTS

WE GIVE SPECIAL THANKS . . .

To our current and former colleagues in Research Services, Presbyterian Church (U.S.A.): Keith Wulff (coordinator), Charlene Briggs, Sarahjoy Crewe, Rebecca Farnham, Charisse LeMaster, John P. Marcum, Olga Mayorova, Amy Noh, Ida Smith-Williams, Janice Spang, and Jamie Spence.

To our research colleagues who directed the denominational oversamples: Roger Dudley, Bryan Froehle, Mary Gautier, Kirk Hadaway, Richard Houseal, Phil Jones, Matthew Price, Marty Smith, and Craig This.

To other colleagues who served as consultants to the project: Steve Boots, Kenneth Byerly, Jackson Carroll, Keith Castle, Mark Chavez, Michael Cieslak, Ann Diebert, Robert Dixon, Carl Dudley, Trey Hammond, Dean Hoge, Herb Miller, Becky McMillan, David Roozen, Tom Smith, and Doug Wilson.

To our Australian colleagues who founded the National Church Life Survey and cast the vision for an international project: Peter Kaldor and Dean Drayton.

To our funding organizations and their officers: Chris Coble, of Lilly Endowment Inc., and James Lewis, of the Louisville Institute.

To the congregations who tested and piloted our work as well as the people and organizations too many to name who helped us accomplish this monumental feat.

Finally, to the worshipers and their congregations who generously gave their time to help us portray American religious life at the turn of the century. This guide is their story. May others learn from their voices.

CHAPTER 1

WHY A FIELD GUIDE?

We recently received two highly unusual field guides as gifts: One guide contained everything you could possibly want to know about cows; the other book recounted in detail everything about sport-utility vehicles, or SUVs. The guides were amusing and interesting. But these gifts raised a question for us: Why do we know *less* about U.S. congregations than we do about cows and SUVs? Aren't congregations, as one of the most enduring expressions of American religious life, just as important to comprehend as our automobiles and livestock? A search of bookstore shelves under "Field Guides" yielded more examples of research describing birds, plants, and animals. As researchers committed to understanding religion in America, we decided a field guide to congregations would add an important volume to the shelf.

America has always been known for its voluntary associations of all types. Research documenting how voluntary groups make use of resources, especially volunteers, abounds. Recent attention has focused on how voluntary groups respond to larger cultural changes as well as to their more specific contexts. The most common and enduring of all voluntary organizations is the local church or congregation. When compared to other associations, congregations exhibit incredible strength and vitality. No other voluntary organization enjoys the degree of commitment and centrality in the life of its "volunteers" as does the local church or congregation. In fact, the depth of many members' and worshipers' commitment makes leaders and others sometimes forget that they indeed are volunteers. And these volunteers can and do vote with their feet!

What is unique about the congregation as a voluntary association? Congregations are like clay creatures—inventions of our own making, part of the social fabric, fulfilling quite ordinary human needs. Congregations are like common clay in another way because they possess the uncommon qualities of both extreme resiliency and fragility. We've heard stories about congregations and parishes that rose from the ashes—they were down to their last five members or their building was destroyed by fire, and they found a way to be reborn, stronger in mission than ever before. Others tell stories of David-like congregations slaying the Goliaths of poverty, despair, or injustice in their communities. We also recognize the stories of strong congregations, perhaps with thousands of members, destroyed by problematic personalities, theological splits, or other unnatural disasters—all signs of the paradoxical fragility and resiliency of congregational life.

Yet these vessels of clay are quite uncommon. They embody the sacred in an increasingly secular world. They demonstrate God's creative work in the world. Just as humans are clay creatures, filled with God's own breath, so congregations carry the breath of the divine in a hurting world. If we want to help congregations and parishes, don't we need to better understand this uncommon nature? If we are committed to the task of strengthening congregations and their leaders, aren't we partners with God in an uncommon calling?

Can We See More from the Pews?

Many people say they know what American worshipers find meaningful in a congregation. Reputable experts compile lists of qualities they believe contribute to "congregational vitality." Books advise congregations and parishes about priorities they should emphasize. Yet until now, little evidence has existed that paints an accurate picture of the American religious landscape.

Most worshipers believe their congregation is unique. In many ways they are right. Every congregation is a collection of one-of-a-kind individuals who make up a distinct group portrait. Each congregation's location is also unique: on a particular street, in a particular neighborhood, in a one-of-a-kind city or town or rural community. Certainly, the singular setting of a congregation shapes it in ways we do not fully understand. However, congregational leaders often use this uniqueness as an excuse for ignoring lessons that they can learn from others. Thus, changes that might increase their congregation's effectiveness never are heard.

While each congregation is unique, much about congregations is universal. Congregations share similar dreams and struggles. Committed to that vision, the authors worked with research teams from Australia, New Zealand, and England to study congregations and parishes. The study results you hold in your hands were replicated in three other countries. This international effort recognized the hopes and dreams of 1.2 million worshipers in 12,000 congregations. The creative interplay of these researchers, who are committed to helping congregations, sharpened our focus: *Who attends religious services? Why do they go? What makes American congregations and parishes work? What is the role of our culture and society in shaping the nature of congregations?* This volume is the first step in describing "what is" and "who we are" in American congregations.

Why now? Many participants, stakeholders, and congregation watchers have a sense that we are in an "in-between" time—not too far from the past when most denominations and congregations were growing and the number of priests, pastors, and

MYTH TRAPS

Myths are tempting assumptions about congregational life. Just as cheese lures a mouse, myths lure us to beliefs we want to be true. Believing myths is its own reward. Myths allow us to avoid change. Myths permit us to use the same old methods to get the same old results. Myths immobilize and trap us in dead ends, blocking us from fully living out the answer to our most important question: What is God calling us to be and do as a congregation?

ministers met the demand. But we are certainly not fully in the future where present challenges have grounded new creativity in ministry. In this transition time, shifting from past to future, a general sense of unease prevails. Many leaders believe that some congregations are in denial about present-day realities. Other parishes and congregations that have moved beyond denial now face despair. Should leaders move forward to discernment, decision making, and action? Can we use our discomfort as motivation to open the door to new possibilities? We believe so.

Leading congregations has never been more difficult. The tasks and obstacles have never been more complex. Organizational problems, changes in the community, and rising expectations often undermine efforts by the most talented and charismatic of leaders. People demand better results from every institution they encounter, including their congregation and parish. Congregational leaders need the kind of reality-based organizational analysis that business leaders in growing, healthy, excellence-oriented companies find helpful. This volume offers a similar reality-based view for religious leaders and worshipers.

The U.S. Congregational Life Survey

The scope of the U.S. Congregational Life Survey project is immense. Funded by generous grants from Lilly Endowment Inc. and the Louisville Institute, the national study provides the largest and most representative profile of worshipers and their congregations ever developed in the United States. More than 300,000 worshipers filled out a survey during religious services in April 2001. (See appendix 1 for more details.)

The survey project explored four dimensions of congregational life—spirituality and faith development; activities and relationships within the congregation; community involvement; and worshipers' vision for the congregation's future. Chapter 3 examines the ways congregations and parishes help people grow in their faith through their worship life and other congregational activities. A second important area of congregational life—what happens inside the congregation—is reported in chapter 4. That chapter reports worshipers' participation in congregational groups, their sense of belonging, and their leadership roles. Community involvement is investigated in chapter 5, including services that congregations provide to the community and efforts to invite people to worship services and other congregational activities. Chapter 6 details some specific types of worshipers, such as frequent attendees and first-time attendees. Finally, the study findings in chapter 7 capture worshipers' views about the future directions of their congregation.

How Is This Picture Different from What You've Seen Before?

The chapters that follow provide a view of the American religious landscape that is different from traditional views in a number of ways:

- ■ *A large representative national sample of congregations and parishes participated in the study.* Previous studies of congregational life have been based on small samples or in-depth case studies. Because congregations involved in these previous studies may not be typical, results are not representative of all congregations. The U.S. Congregational Life Survey polled worshipers from every state across the country.

- ■ *We asked the opinions of both leaders and worshipers.* Most previous studies have relied on the views and opinions of clergy or a single lay leader in participating congregations and parishes. The U.S. Congregational Life Survey records the voices of 300,000 people who regularly invest in congregational life through their participation in worship. Together with information from clergy, their views are the definitive source of information about congregations and parishes.

- ■ *A broad range of denominations and faith groups took part.* Advice offered by consultants and other experts on congregational life is based on years of experience working with congregations. However, their observations are often limited to the range of congregations and parishes encountered in their work.

GUIDELINES

Knowing is not the same thing as doing. People who know a fact do not always apply it. Information or knowledge does not automatically produce change. Unless crucial research facts lead to the question, "If this is true, then what should our congregation do?" the new information becomes interesting but irrelevant. In each chapter, the Guidelines box provides signposts for congregations moving toward data-driven decisions. In view of the presented research facts in each chapter, the reader should ask, "What one or two steps could our congregation take to be more effective in its ministry?"

This scientific research supplements these perspectives by offering a current snapshot of congregations based on a random sample of U.S. congregations. It provides an opportunity for all of us to test our own theories and the experiential advice being offered by consultants and denominational leaders.

■ *Congregational health is envisioned as more than numerical growth.* Rather than relying on one measure of vitality, we investigated four fundamental areas of congregational life—spirituality and faith development; involvement in groups and leadership roles; community involvement; and future directions. Thus, congregations and parishes can see where their strengths are and where change may be needed in the multidimensional arena of vitality.

■ *The experiences of worshipers in congregations of all sizes are included.* Too often researchers and congregational consultants select large congregations or mega-churches, rapidly growing congregations, congregations with one-of-a-kind ministries, congregations in conflict, or congregations and parishes that are unique in some other way. This causes difficulties for leaders and attendees who attempt to apply the lessons in small or mid-sized congregations, in declining or stable communities, or in other settings. The findings complement and qualify the congregational examples found elsewhere.

Many researchers see the search for common threads in congregational life across the diversity of U.S. faith communities as an impossible mission. Yet we believe there are common questions that all congregations and parishes face: Who are we? What is our mission? What do we believe? Do we welcome others? How do we do so? How do we relate to the community? How do we adapt to change while maintaining our core values? While the search for general trends is a difficult one, it is an essential requirement for congregations seeking to look more closely at their health and vitality.

The Case for Data-Driven Decisions

Many factors can and should drive a congregation's decisions. Among those factors, leaders in various denominations and faith traditions use four with great frequency:

- *Theology-driven decisions.* For example, a congregation or parish believes in a God whose nature calls them to minister with refugees, people with HIV/AIDS, or other caring actions.

- *Bible-driven decisions.* For example, a congregation believes in the Great Commandment and the Great Commission, which encourages compassionate efforts to help people in the community and invites others to a life-changing and personal relationship with Jesus Christ.

- *Spirit-driven decisions.* For example, a congregation believes in seeking and deriving direction from prayer or discernment that comes from a sense of being led by God's spirit.

- *Tradition-driven decisions.* For example, a congregation believes in a high level of support to worldwide missionary efforts or intensive efforts to end racism in the community. These actions stem from the congregation's heritage or how the congregation has always done things in the past.

A fifth factor can influence a congregation's decisions—information or data. Unfortunately, many congregations make fewer data-driven decisions than their current reality requires, depending instead on other factors, such as the four described above. What happens if a congregation or parish leaves out of its decision-making equation information about the changed nature of the community in which they are located? What happens if a congregation ignores the data that reveal a change in its congregational leadership and identity? These congregations move faithfully forward making decisions based on nonexistent realities. Moving forward on used-to-be truths or half-truths produces disappointing and sometimes disastrous outcomes.

Congregations operate out of mental maps based on a complex mix of these and other factors. These mental maps direct congregations as much as road maps direct the traveler. The destination points and plotted highways leaders have constructed for congregational life send them on guardedly charted journeys that too often are resource consuming and unsatisfying. What if parish and congregational leaders revised their mental maps? What if they made new maps based on an accurate picture of the current landscape?

Who Speaks for Congregations?

Reality matters, and what people do with facts matters even more. The Tacoma Narrows Bridge built over Puget Sound, Washington, collapsed only four months after it was constructed. What happened? At the time, the reason for the collapse was a mystery. When engineers and architects studied the bridge and determined "nothing was wrong," they decided to rebuild the bridge in exactly the same way. Theodore von Kármán, a distinguished Hungarian-born physics professor, heard of the decision and warned the builders that if they rebuilt the bridge in the same way, the span would fall again. His recommendation was based on an understanding of moderate winds—a harmonic principle known today as "von Kármán's vortex." Initially his warning was met with suspicion and skepticism. Looking for ulterior motives, they asked him: "What is your interest in this? Who do you represent? For whom do you speak?"

In his rich Hungarian accent, von Kármán replied: "I speak for the wind."[1]

Who speaks for congregations? Facts matter! Basing actions on an accurate assessment of reality is critical. This book invites leaders and worshipers to gain a fresh perspective on which to base congregational thinking, priorities, planning, and action.

1. Remarks by Paul C. O'Brien, chairman of New England Telephone, Newcoming Society award ceremony, printed in *The Executive Speaker*, February 1995.

CHAPTER 2

Who Worships Where?

In 1934 Roger Tory Peterson developed the "Peterson System" to identify live birds from a distance. Peterson's precise drawings and schematic illustrations replaced the shotgun as the primary tool for noting the unique field marks of each species. What are field marks? For birds, field marks are their "trademarks of nature"—color, tail and wing patterns, and rump patches—distinguishing one species from another. What are the field marks of worshipers or congregations? What specific features tag their common nature? Just as bird-watchers rely on accurate drawings, the following field marks of congregations and their worshipers can instruct serious observers of American religious life.

How to Identify a Worshiper

People who attend religious services in a church, synagogue, or temple exhibit unique traits. These worshipers differ from the average American in several ways. What are their field marks?[1]

---

1. For more detail about how we surveyed worshipers across America, see appendix 1. All percentages are rounded to the nearest whole number. As a result, responses for some questions will total 99% or 101%. This is a standard convention in social scientific survey reporting.

Men or women? There are fewer men (39%) in worship than women (61%).[2] Since the U.S. Census Bureau reports that 51% of the U.S. population is female, this means that women are more often drawn to congregational life than men. In fact, there are more women than men in the pews in every age category. Among worshipers over 65 years of age, women account for 63%. Of course, this is partly because women live longer than men by an average of 5 years. The smallest gender gap between worshipers is among people between 15 and 24 years of age. In this age group, the percentage of women worshipers exceeds male worshipers by only 14%. (See Figure 2.1.)

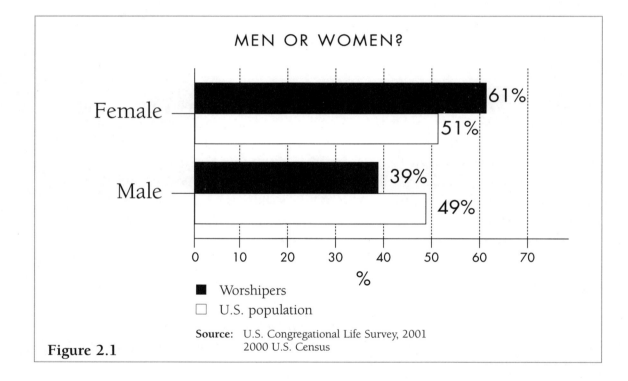

Figure 2.1

2. Because the survey was completed by worshipers 15 years of age and older, all the statistics in the book refer only to people in that age group. For example, if the text says 50% of worshipers have a particular trait, it means that 50% of all worshipers 15 years of age and older have that characteristic. It tells us nothing about the

How old are they? The average age of a worshiper is 50 years. (Remember: We're only talking about the average age of those 15 years of age and older.) The country's average age is only 44 years. Thus, the average worshiper is older by almost 6 years than the average American. Among worshipers, those between the ages of 45 and 64 (36%) are the biggest group. (See Figure 2.2.)

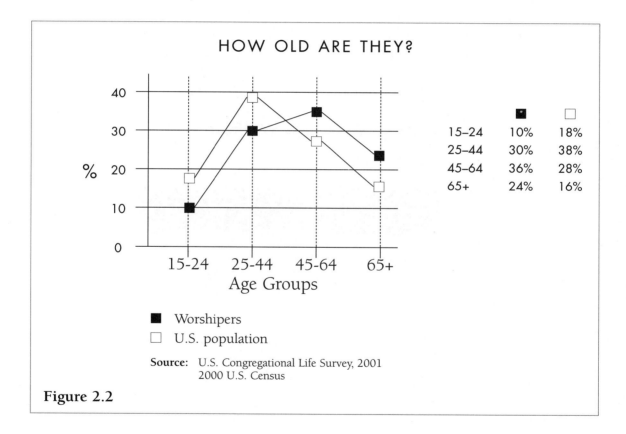

Figure 2.2

---

common features of worshipers less than 15 years of age. In the same way, to make comparisons between worshipers and the American population, information from the U.S. Census Bureau also refers only to Americans 15 years of age and older.

Do they work outside the home? Half of all worshipers (58%) are employed full- or part-time. Compared to the U.S. population, worshipers are more likely to be retired. In fact, one in four worshipers (25%) are retired, which is much higher than the average of 14% for all Americans. Obviously, the larger percentage of retired worshipers is related to the large percentage of older worshipers. One in ten worshipers describe themselves as homemakers. Students make up 9% of all worshipers.

How much education do they have? Worshipers in the U.S. tend to be well educated. The U.S. Census reports that across the country about 23% of the population has a college degree or higher education. The Census reports this figure for people 25 years

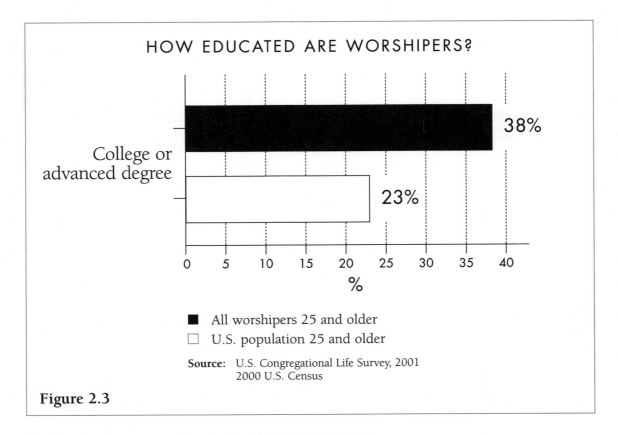

HOW EDUCATED ARE WORSHIPERS?

College or advanced degree
- 38%
- 23%

%

■ All worshipers 25 and older
□ U.S. population 25 and older

Source: U.S. Congregational Life Survey, 2001
2000 U.S. Census

Figure 2.3

of age or older. Among worshipers 25 years of age or older, the figure is 38%. This percentage climbs to 46% for attendees less than 65 years of age. Fully 87% of all worshipers have completed high school. (See Figure 2.3.)

What is their annual income? People in the pews come from all walks of life. One in four worshipers earns less than $25,000 a year. Another one-third earns between $50,000 and $100,000 a year, with 15% earning $100,000 or more a year. Nine percent earn less than $10,000 a year. The U.S. Census reports the median household income is $41,343. Among worshipers, the average is $37,500. (See Figure 2.4.)

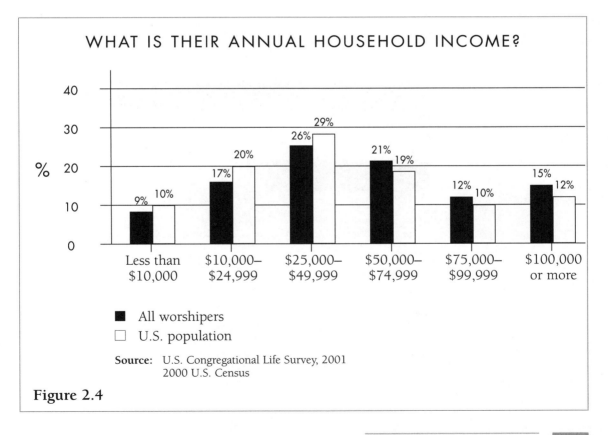

Figure 2.4

WHAT IS THEIR ANNUAL HOUSEHOLD INCOME?

All worshipers
U.S. population

Source: U.S. Congregational Life Survey, 2001
2000 U.S. Census

Are they married? Most worshipers in America are married (66%)—and most of these in their first marriage (55% of all worshipers are in their first marriage). Just over a tenth (11%) have remarried after divorce or the death of a spouse. Congregational participants are therefore much more likely to be married than the average person (52% of the U.S. population are married). Only 8% are separated or divorced compared to a national figure of 11%. A small number of attendees (2%) are living together in a committed relationship other than marriage. The largest group of single people in congregational life consists of those who have never been married. They make up 16% of people in the pews. (See Figure 2.5.)

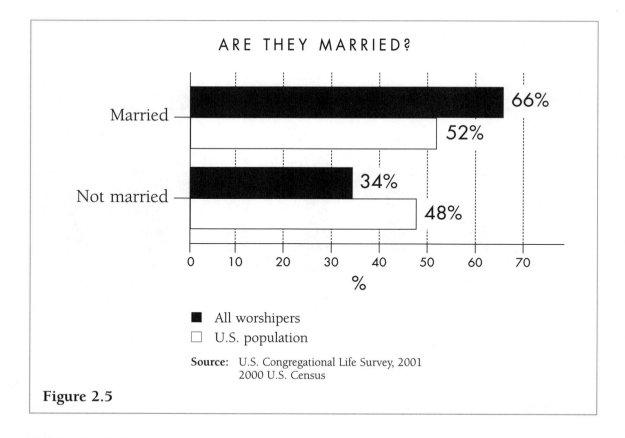

Figure 2.5

Do worshipers attend services alone? Half of the people who completed the survey during worship services said they were attending with their spouse or partner.

Do they have children? Another area of dramatic difference between worshipers and the general public relates to children in the home. People with kids are more likely to go to church or to religious services. Almost half of all worshipers (47%) have children living at home. In the U.S. population, the comparable percentage is only 33%. The second-largest household type (39%) is adults living together, whether married or unrelated. About 14% live alone.

What is their race and ethnicity? Worshipers are similar to other Americans in terms of the proportion who are white, Hispanic, or Asian. More than three out of four worshipers (78%) are white (compared to 72% of the U.S. population). Hispanics (13%) were the second-largest ethnic group in the study (compared to 12% in the U.S. population). Four percent of worshipers are Asian, again an almost identical percentage as in the general population. While 12% of the U.S. population are African Americans, only 5% of the surveys were completed by African American worshipers.

Where were they born? Throughout American history, new immigrant groups have found their place of worship to be a source of support in a new and alien land. Their congregations and parishes provided a place where native languages and customs could be continued and networks of families and friends maintained. More than one in eight worshipers (13%) were *not* born in the United States. The majority of foreign-born worshipers (70%) were born in non-English-speaking countries.

Location, location, location. The trip to worship is a short one. Half of all worshipers can get to religious services in just 10 minutes or less. Almost all (88%) can get to their

MYTH TRAP

People under 30 do not participate in religious activities.

Given the large gap between the average worshiper and the average age in the U.S. population, it is easy to conclude that religious activities attract only older adults. However, many congregations are filled with worshipers under 30. What are these congregations offering that younger adults find meaningful?

congregation's site in 20 minutes or less. The worshiper who travels 30 minutes or more is a rare person. Only 4% of the participants travel for more than half an hour to attend services.

How to Identify a Congregation

Many voluntary organizations flourish in America, from the Rotary Club to book clubs, from intramural sports teams to professional organizations, from neighborhood homeowners' associations to sororities and fraternities. What have more than 2,000 participating congregations told us about themselves to help us identify congregations and distinguish them from other voluntary organizations?

How large? Congregational size can be determined in several ways.[3] The largest figures were reported when we asked about the total number of people associated *in any way* with the congregation—this includes adults and children, members and nonmembers, regular participants and infrequent attendees. The average (median) congregation or parish size using this yardstick was 200. Looking at people who *regularly* participate in the congregation reduces the average to 110. Further restricting the view to worshipers aged 18 and older who regularly participate brings the average down to 80. We also asked about the average attendance in worship (which would often include teenagers and children) and found an average of 90 people. (See Figure 2.6.)

What is the congregation's affiliation? A large majority of congregations (88%) cite an affiliation with a denomination, convention, or other association. Baptist churches make up the largest group (23% of all congregations, including 16% affiliated with the Southern Baptist Convention). Other denominational groups with many participating congregations include: Methodists (14% overall, almost all of which are part of the United Methodist Church), Roman Catholic parishes (11%), and Lutheran churches (11% overall, including 8% that are affiliated with the Evangelical Lutheran Church in America). Yet a wide variety of denominations are included in the study, from Mennonites to Unitarians, from Orthodox Jews to African Methodist Episcopalians. (Appendix 2 provides the complete list.)

---

3. The results in this section come not from the responses of individual worshipers but rather from a congregational profile completed by one leader in each congregation. The profile provided information about the facilities, programs, finances, and staff of each congregation.

HOW LARGE ARE U.S. CONGREGATIONS?

	Median
Number of people associated in any way with the congregation	200
Number of people regularly participating in the congregation	110
Number of adults (18 and up) regularly participating in the congregation	80
Average worship attendance	90

Figure 2.6

Where does the congregation worship? A large majority of congregations and parishes (90%) hold their primary worship service in a church building—not surprising given the affiliation of participating congregations. Others worship in synagogues, temples, school buildings, store fronts, and community centers. Most own their own facilities (94%). The remainder rent space or meet for free in a building owned by others. On average, the space where a congregation's largest worship service is held seats about 200 people, but the range of sizes is impressive—the smallest space seats 40 and the largest seats 3,000.

How is the congregation financially supported? Almost all congregations and parishes (99%) list individual contributions (in the form of offerings, pledges, donations, or dues) as one of the three biggest sources of income. One-quarter also cite income from trust funds, investments, or bequests. Another 16% report income from charges for use of the congregation's facilities or buildings.

The median congregational income from all sources is about $105,000 annually and ranges from a low of $650 to a high of over $9 million. Congregational expenses (including salaries, debt service, money sent to the denomination or other religious organizations, and all other purposes) average just $5,500 less than the average income. Operating expenses alone average about $84,000 annually. Thus, the typical congregation spends most of its income on day-to-day operating expenses and a much smaller portion on program and mission. (See Figure 2.7.)

When asked to describe the congregation's financial situation, half reported that the congregation has an essentially stable financial base, and 29% enjoy an increasing financial base. The remaining congregations are not so fortunate—16% overall have a declining base, and 2% face a financial situation that is a serious threat to their continued existence.

How is the congregation staffed? All but 8% of congregations have at least some paid staff. Most (79%) have at least one full-time ordained professional staff person, and in fact 65% have just one such person on staff. About half have part-time custodial or maintenance staff. One-quarter of congregations employ clerical staff on a full-time basis, and one-third do so on a part-time basis. Other categories of employees (for example, lay professionals, day-care or school employees) are reported by smaller percentages of congregations.

How old is the congregation? Few participating congregations were founded recently—just 13% were established in the last 20 years. Rather, many have stood the test of time—one-third are more than 100 years old, and the average (median) age is 73 years.

HOW IS THE CONGREGATION FINANCIALLY SUPPORTED?

	Median Amount For Most Recent Fiscal Year
Income from all sources	$105,180
Income from individuals' donations, dues, or contributions	$88,450
Total congregation budget	$99,610
Congregation's operating expenses	$83,940

Figure 2.7

What Does Typical Mean?

Why does Alison, who attends a mega-church of 5,000 with multiple weekend services, find the above description of congregational life hard to believe? Why does Keith, who participates in a mainline Protestant congregation of 350, also wonder why the illustrations in this chapter do not match his experiences? The answer: Alison and Keith, as *typical* worshipers, find themselves in congregations of larger-than-average size. A wide gap exists between where the largest numbers of people worship and the size of the typical congregation. Most congregations are small. But most worshipers are in large congregations.

Imagine a small town of 1,000 people. This town has 10 congregations of various faith groups—Catholic, Protestant, and other religions. If all worshipers were equally spread among the congregations, each congregation would have 100 members (assuming everyone in town attends religious services!). But this is not the case. For example, one of the congregations is a Catholic parish. Since Catholics are organized geographically into parishes, all the Catholics in town would go to the Catholic church. Because Catholics make up 25% of the population, 250 people would be attending Mass there. That leaves only 750 people in town as potential worshipers for the other nine congregations. Are the 750 people spread out evenly among the remaining nine congregations? Probably not. One congregation may have a charismatic leader, a wonderful program for children and youth, or a new building. They average 350 people in worship every week. Quite a crowd in this small town! Now only 400 people are left to attend services at the other eight congregations. If each of these eight congregations got their "fair share," it would mean they attract only 50 worshipers each! While eight out of the ten *congregations* are small, the other reality is that 60% of the *people* in this imaginary town worship in a large church, synagogue, or temple.

How do these factors play out in communities across America? Some congregations enjoy a large attendance at their services because of their faith tradition, their exemplary services or programs, or other features. Thus, the *typical* worshiper experiences a large congregation. This does not change the fact that the average congregation has fewer than 100 people in worship.

Explaining the gap between what typical congregations look like and what typical worshipers experience is difficult. As our mythical town illustrates, the distribution of congregations is vastly different from the spread of worshipers across those congregations. A parallel example might be where typical dollars are found. The typical dollar belongs to a wealthy household, but the typical household has few dollars!

Another way to summarize this gap is with the following facts: 10% of U.S. congregations draw 50% of all worshipers each week. Another 40% of congregations have 39% of worshipers attending services that week. The remaining 50% of all congregations have only 11% of the total number of worshipers in a given week.

Finally, unlike the imaginary town, not all Americans associate with a faith community or congregation. Only 45% of the population is claimed by a denomination or faith group.[4] Further, only 21% of the population reports attending worship services in the previous week.[5] Small congregations or congregations of any size in any community will find many people who do not regularly attend worship services outside their doors.

What Matters?

The field marks illustrated in this chapter help leaders and others begin to identify the unique characteristics of their worshipers and congregation. People who worship together differ from other Americans in profound ways. Worshipers are more educated, with large percentages holding college degrees. More women than men participate in congregational life. Whites and the middle class are more often found attending services than the poor or racial-ethnic minorities. However, some recent immigrants find their worshiping community a bridge to surviving life in a new country.

Much about U.S. congregations and parishes is determined by their key characteristics—affiliation, size, and resource base. Congregations are not evenly distributed across the various faith groups. This means that, in a given community, there may be several congre-

---

4. M. B. Bradley et al., *Churches and Church Membership in the United States, 1990* (Atlanta: Glenmary Research Center, 1992).

5. K. Hadaway and P. Marler, "It All Depends on How You Ask the Question: Item Wording and Self-Reported Church Attendance in Three Nations" (presentation at the Society for the Scientific Study of Religion, Columbus, Oh., October 2001).

gations of one faith group (e.g., conservative Protestant) but no congregations representing other types. Some small denominations or faith groups have limited resources to start new congregations or to support struggling existing ones. The number of congregations associated with a denomination or faith group directly affects worshipers who move to a new community hoping to find a congregation like the one they left. If the denomination is small, their new community may not have a congregation of their faith tradition.

Most congregations have fewer than 100 people in worship services. This key fact of congregational life has far-reaching consequences. With so few people, raising funds and supporting full-time clergy or other professional staff can pose problems. Most congregations and parishes also own their own building. Again, with fewer than 100 people to fund the expense of upkeep and operation of their facilities, resources are taxed. Day-to-day operating expenses may leave little money to fund extensive programs, community services, or other ministry projects.

A considerable gap often exists between the number of members a congregation has and the number of people who regularly attend services. Worship attendance figures tend to give a more realistic picture of the actual community life and resource base of a congregation. Typically, worship attendance on any given day is about 50% of the membership. All too often congregations have their identity "fixed" on the size of their membership rather than on the number of worshipers. The larger this perception gap is for a congregation, the more likely it is that it needs a new prescription to focus on new directions.

GUIDELINES

A typical worshiper is . . .

- female
- 50 years old
- employed
- well educated
- married
- white

Does this describe our typical worshiper? Who does this profile of a typical worshiper leave out? Who is in our community or parish but not participating in our services and activities? What one or two steps could our congregation take to invite, welcome, and include new people in our worshiping community?

The congregation was evenly split between those that mooed in worship and those that baaed.

CHAPTER 3

SPIRITUAL CONNECTIONS

The next three chapters of this field guide describe several of the conceptual building blocks for understanding the complex nature of congregational life: spiritual connections, inside connections, and outside connections. The complexity of these connections illustrates a key lesson from research: congregational life is rarely about one or two variables. Because these dimensions of congregational life are interrelated, dynamics in one place will directly affect all other areas. Where is the best place to begin? Since congregations and parishes primarily focus on worshipers' encounters with God and the sacred, spiritual connections are explored first in this chapter.

What Are Spiritual Connections?

Congregations cultivate faith and respond to the religious needs of worshipers. Spiritual growth for individual worshipers can result from private devotional activities, participation in worship services or other congregational activities, or participation in activities of other groups or organizations. The spiritual lives of worshipers and the worship activities of their congregations are described below.

Private devotions: How often do worshipers pray, meditate, or read the Bible? The majority of worshipers (63%) spend at least a few times a week in such activities. A large percentage (45%) spend time *every day* in prayer, meditation, reading the Bible, or other private, devotional activities. People attending Catholic parishes spend time in private devotional activities less often than worshipers in other types of congregations. (See Figure 3.1.)

Growing in faith? Half of all worshipers (54%) say they have experienced much growth in their faith during the last year. What fostered their growth in faith? One in three attribute their spiritual growth to their participation in the congregation, 15%

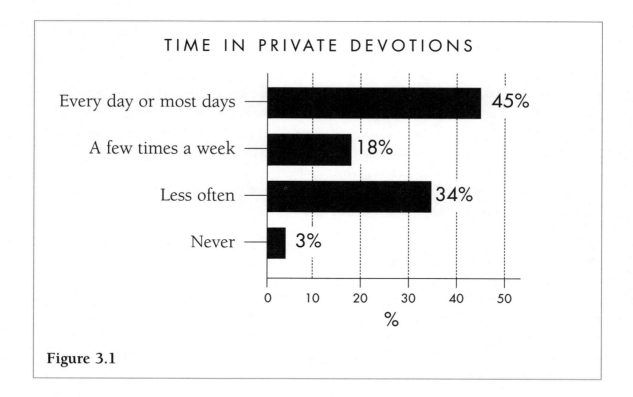

Figure 3.1

attribute it to their own private activities, and only a few (7%) attribute it to their involvement in other groups or congregations. Surprisingly, almost half report that they either had experienced only some growth in faith (39%) or had not grown in their faith in the last year (7%). Catholic worshipers are less likely to credit their parish involvement as the source of their spiritual growth and somewhat more likely to credit their personal activities. (See Figure 3.2.)

Rating the congregation or parish: Is it meeting worshipers' spiritual needs? Worshipers give their congregations high marks for meeting their spiritual needs. The majority (83%) believe their spiritual needs are being met through their congregation or parish.

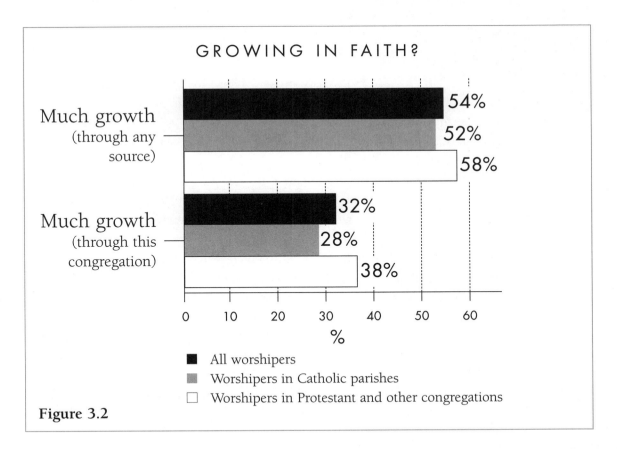

GROWING IN FAITH?

Much growth
(through any
source)
- 54% — All worshipers
- 52% — Worshipers in Catholic parishes
- 58% — Worshipers in Protestant and other congregations

Much growth
(through this
congregation)
- 32% — All worshipers
- 28% — Worshipers in Catholic parishes
- 38% — Worshipers in Protestant and other congregations

%

■ All worshipers
▨ Worshipers in Catholic parishes
□ Worshipers in Protestant and other congregations

Figure 3.2

Another sign of satisfaction. Almost all rate the worship services or congregational activities as helpful to everyday living: 45% say their congregation or parish helps them with their daily living "to a great extent," and another 41% say "to some extent."

Conversion or not? They've not seen the light. For most worshipers, the faith experience is a long-term process of growing commitment. One in five worshipers describe their faith commitment as a gradual process. Half of all worshipers say they have had faith for as long as they can remember. Worshipers in Catholic parishes are especially likely to report that their faith has always been a part of their life. Among all worshipers, fewer than one in three can point to a definite moment of commitment or conversion. Worshipers in Protestant churches and congregations of other faith groups are more likely to cite a definite moment of commitment or a conversion experience (34%) than those in Catholic parishes (23%). (See Figure 3.3.)

One Book but many views: Views of the Bible. Differing views about the Bible underlie many theological and denominational policy debates. Worshipers were presented with six general statements about the Bible. The statement most often identified by worshipers (42%) as representing their own views was "The Bible is the Word of God, to be interpreted in the light of its historical context and the Church's teachings." Less than one-third of all worshipers (28%) embrace a more literal understanding of the Bible ("The Bible is the Word of God, to be taken literally word for word"). One in five chose the statement that reflects a mainline Protestant view of the Bible ("The Bible is the Word of God, to be interpreted in the light of its historical and cultural context"). Less than 6% hold a view of the Bible that does not recognize it as the Word of God. Some (3%) even confessed that they don't know how they view the Bible. (See Figure 3.4.)

Two distinct views of the Bible emerge when comparing worshipers in Catholic parishes to other worshipers. The majority in Catholic parishes (53%) agreed with the

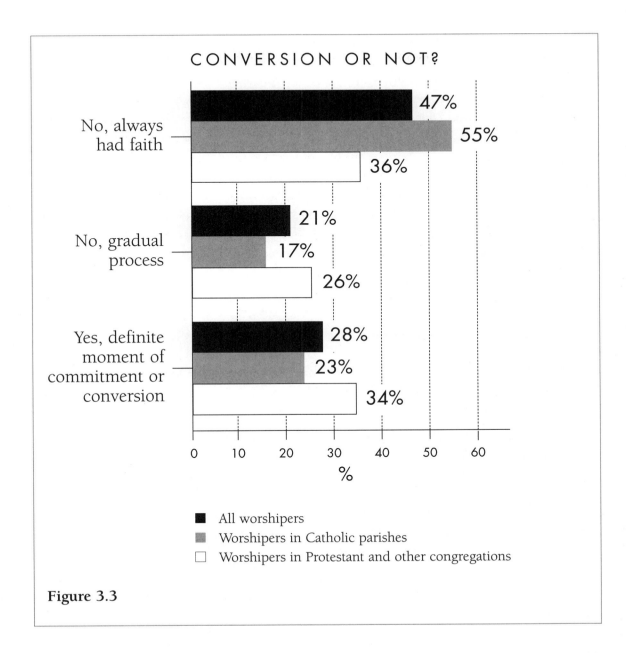

CONVERSION OR NOT?

No, always had faith
- All worshipers: 47%
- Worshipers in Catholic parishes: 55%
- Worshipers in Protestant and other congregations: 36%

No, gradual process
- All worshipers: 21%
- Worshipers in Catholic parishes: 17%
- Worshipers in Protestant and other congregations: 26%

Yes, definite moment of commitment or conversion
- All worshipers: 28%
- Worshipers in Catholic parishes: 23%
- Worshipers in Protestant and other congregations: 34%

%

■ All worshipers
  Worshipers in Catholic parishes
□ Worshipers in Protestant and other congregations

Figure 3.3

following statement about the Bible: "The Bible is the Word of God, to be interpreted in the light of its historical context and the Church's teachings." Other worshipers (40%) were more likely to identify with a literal interpretation of the sacred text: "The Bible is the Word of God, to be taken literally word for word."

"I like mine, but they're all good." Half of all worshipers take a relativist stance toward religion—that is, they believe "all the different religions are equally good ways of helping a person find ultimate truth." Almost one-third disagreed with this statement, and some (18%) were neutral or unsure about it.

How do people experience the worship services of their congregation? Most say they feel a sense of God's presence during worship and experience joy and inspiration. Some report that they gain a sense of fulfilling their obligations by attending worship. It is less common for people to say they experience awe, mystery, or spontaneity as they

---

VIEWS OF THE BIBLE

Which statement comes closest to your view of the Bible? (Mark *one* only.)

The Bible is the Word of God, to be taken literally word for word. 28%

The Bible is the Word of God, to be interpreted in the light of its
historical and cultural context 20%

The Bible is the Word of God, to be interpreted in the light of its
historical context and the church's teachings 42%

The Bible is not the Word of God, but contains God's Word to us 4%

The Bible is not the Word of God but is a valuable book 1%

The Bible is an ancient book with little value today . . . . *

Don't know 3%

* = less than 0.5%; rounds to zero

Figure 3.4

---

worship. Thankfully, most people do not have a negative experience, such as boredom or frustration. (See Figure 3.5.)

Hymns top the charts. The majority of worshipers (61%) prefer traditional hymns over other styles of music during congregational worship. One in three (33%) prefer praise music or choruses, and 25% prefer contemporary hymns. (Note: Worshipers could choose up to two styles of music.) Other styles of music are preferred by fewer people—contemporary music other than hymns (13%), sung responsorial psalms (10%), classical music (9%), music or songs from a variety of cultures (9%), African American gospel (5%), and contemplative chants (2%). (See Figure 3.6.)

Worship as the Main Event

The spiritual lives of attendees are further enriched by their experiences with others in worship. What are congregations offering to participants? How do congregations organize these regular opportunities to experience the sacred?

When and how many services? It's no longer just a once-a-week Sunday morning affair, and for some faith traditions it never was! *Two-thirds* of congregations offer more than one worship service in a typical week. These services may be on Saturday or Friday or Monday, but most are on Sunday. Of course, some faith traditions have had a history of more than one Sunday worship service. For example, Southern Baptists traditionally had a morning service as well as an evening service, and faithful worshipers were expected to attend both. Many congregations, however, have abandoned this practice. Multiple services, especially over a weekend, are often offered to give worshipers a convenient choice of worship times. Roman Catholics have long had these options since, in

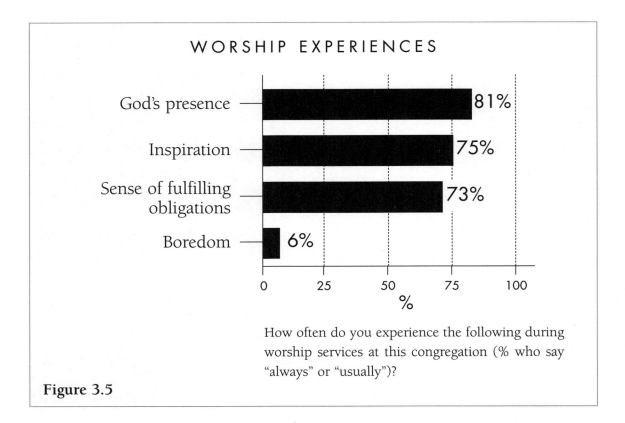

WORSHIP EXPERIENCES

God's presence — 81%

Inspiration — 75%

Sense of fulfilling obligations — 73%

Boredom — 6%

0   25   50   75   100

%

How often do you experience the following during worship services at this congregation (% who say "always" or "usually")?

Figure 3.5

many parishes, Mass is offered daily and a number of times on weekends. Furthermore, Saturday is the sacred day for worship for Seventh-day Adventists and Jews.

We asked congregations to give us specific information for up to five worship services. In all, they told us about 1,017 different services. Three-quarters of these services are held on Sunday. Wednesday and Saturday are also common days for services—14% of services take place on Wednesday and 5% on Saturday.

Most of these services occur weekly (96%), but others are seasonal (for example, services held on Good Friday or other holy days) or periodic (biweekly or monthly). The largest percentage of services (18%) start at 11:00 A.M., and about half start in the period between 9:00 and 11:00 A.M. Three in ten occur at 6:00 P.M. or later.

One-half of these services were described as traditional in style, 14% as contemporary, and 33% as blended. Slightly more than one-third are for nonmembers or "seekers," those searching for a new faith community.

What happens in the typical worship service? In almost all worship services, someone preaches a sermon or homily or gives a speech or talk. The sermon, homily, or speech usually lasts between 11 and 20 minutes, although some worshipers enjoy a stirring hour's worth or more.

Most congregations take an offering or collect money during worship services. Because individual contributions are the major source of income for most congregations, this is a key element.

HYMNS TOP THE CHARTS

While you may value many different styles of music, which of the following do you prefer in congregational worship? (Mark up to *two* options.)

Traditional hymns. 61%

Praise music or choruses. 33%

Contemporary hymns. 25%

Other contemporary music or songs (not hymns). 13%

Sung responsorial psalms 10%

Classical music or chorales 9%

Music or songs from a variety of cultures. 9%

African American gospel music 5%

Contemplative chants (Taizé, Iona) 2%

No music or songs 1%

Don't know 3%

Figure 3.6

THE LARGEST (OR ONLY) WORSHIP SERVICE INCLUDES*:

Sermon, homily, or speech 100%

Taking up a collection of money 98%

Singing by the congregation 95%

Singing by a choir or soloist 87%

People greeting one another 85%

Hymnbooks 85%

Communion, Eucharist, Lord's Supper. 85%

Length of 1½ hour or less 85%

Piano 84%

Written bulletin or service outline 75%

People speaking, reading, or reciting something together 71%

Laughter. 70%

Special time directed at children 67%

Applause 64%

Organ. 63%

Participation by teens (speaking, singing, performing) 55%

Silent prayer or meditation 54%

*Only those cited by a majority of congregations are shown.

Figure 3.7

Music finds its way into worship services in a variety of ways. In most services, worshipers hear singing in unison by the congregation (often using hymnbooks) and choirs or soloists who perform music. Pianos or organs accompany the service more often than drums or electric guitar.

Communion, the Eucharist, or Lord's Supper is often observed in worship. (See Figure 3.7.)

What kind of music? Traditional hymns are still the most common type of music in most services. Of the 1,012 services congregations described for us, almost three-quarters include traditional hymns. Praise music or choruses are sung in four of ten services, and one-third include contemporary music or hymns. Responsive psalms are common in Catholic parishes but are also used in non-Catholic settings—one-quarter of services overall include such music. Singing in tongues is found in 3% of all services. A few worship services go without—about 7% don't have any music or songs.

This pattern—traditional hymns as most common, followed by praise music and contemporary hymns—mirrors what worshipers say they prefer. Congregations appear to be meeting the music needs of their worshipers. But how do the musical offerings sound to those from outside the faith community who might be considering becoming involved in the congregation? And what impact does the music have on groups who are often underrepresented in congregations—the younger generations, in particular?

What Matters?

For most participants in U.S. congregations, worship is the main event. While some participate in small groups within the congregation or serve the community through the congregation (described in the following chapter), the majority experience the congregation only by attending worship services. Thus, what they get from their religious community must happen during worship. The results here suggest that tremendous care, attention, and planning should be directed at the worship service. Many worshipers are finding the services helpful as they seek to navigate their everyday lives. However, a large percentage say that they attend as a way to fulfill an obligation, and some report that their faith is fostered in venues outside the congregation. Half of all worshipers say they are not growing in their faith. How long will they continue to participate in a faith community if this is the case? Will they continue to participate primarily to fulfill an obligation?

Isabel's contribution to her church community was giving others the opportunity to serve.

CHAPTER 4

INSIDE CONNECTIONS

Field guides note and illustrate the behaviors of the species under scrutiny. While the spiritual experiences covered in the previous chapter are subjective and sometimes difficult to describe, this chapter begins with a focus on the behaviors of worshipers inside the congregation. How do worshipers relate to one another? What activities of the congregation are they involved in beyond worship? This second area of congregational life captures worshipers' involvement in small groups and leadership roles, decision making, and financial contributions. Inside connections also entail how worshipers feel about their relationships with other worshipers. For example, do they feel a strong sense of belonging to their congregation? Do they have friends in the congregation?

Worshiper Behavior

This first section describes what attendees actually do in and with their congregation. Some become official members, join groups, become leaders, or make important decisions on behalf of the congregation. In addition to making a commitment of time, many worshipers commit financially by contributing money to the mission of the parish or congregation.

Becoming a member. One in ten worshipers regularly participate in the congregation but are not members. Another 3% are in the process of becoming members.

Involvement in small groups. Less than half of all worshipers (44%) are involved in small groups organized by the congregation. But worshipers in Protestant churches and congregations of other faith groups are far more likely to be involved in such groups than worshipers in Catholic parishes. Only 30% of those in Catholic parishes are involved in small-group activities. Worshipers in other types of congregations participate at twice this level—62% relate to some type of small group in their congregation. Fellowship groups, clubs, and other social groups associated with the congregation draw the largest group of worshipers (27% overall). Sunday school, church school, or other religious education groups capture 22% of all worshipers. Finally, prayer, discussion, and Bible study groups draw 19% of all worshipers. (Some worshipers participate in more than one type of group.) While worshipers in Catholic parishes report lower levels of involvement with all three types of small groups, the largest gap exists for church or Sunday school (37% for Protestants and others, but only 9% for Catholics). (See Figure 4.1.)

Worshipers as leaders. Four in ten worshipers (38%) serve as leaders in their congregation. These attendees serve on committees, task forces, or the governing board of the congregation; lead or assist in worship; sing in the choir; serve as religious education teachers or church officers; and take on other leadership responsibilities important to congregational life. (See Figure 4.2.)

Again, it is important to note the large difference between worshipers in Catholic parishes and others. Only one in four in Catholic parishes say they hold a leadership position in their parish, while one in two Protestants and others report such a role in their congregation. This large difference results from at least three factors. First, Catholic parishes are large compared to the average size of other congregations. Thus, in Catholic parishes there are simply fewer leadership positions per person in the pew to be filled. Second, the centralized decision-making structure and other polity differences between Catholic parishes and other congregations contribute to a lower number of available leadership roles. Third, other evidence suggests that in fact Catholic worshipers participate in parish life other than attending Mass at lower rates than other denominations or faith groups.

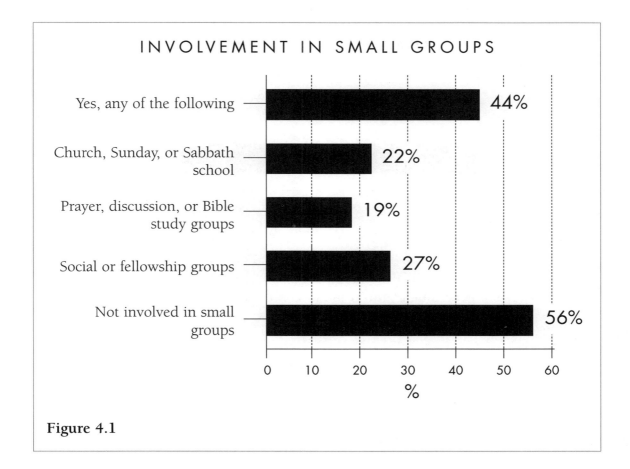

INVOLVEMENT IN SMALL GROUPS

- Yes, any of the following — **44%**
- Church, Sunday, or Sabbath school — **22%**
- Prayer, discussion, or Bible study groups — **19%**
- Social or fellowship groups — **27%**
- Not involved in small groups — **56%**

%

Figure 4.1

Involved in making decisions. While most worshipers say they have been given the opportunity to participate in congregational decision making (68%), only a third (31%) even occasionally do so. More (38%) feel they've been given the opportunity but have chosen not to get involved in important decision making. The final third say they've *not* been given the chance to be decision makers but are happy with the situation as it is. Only 6% expressed any dissatisfaction about not being part of decisions in the congregation.

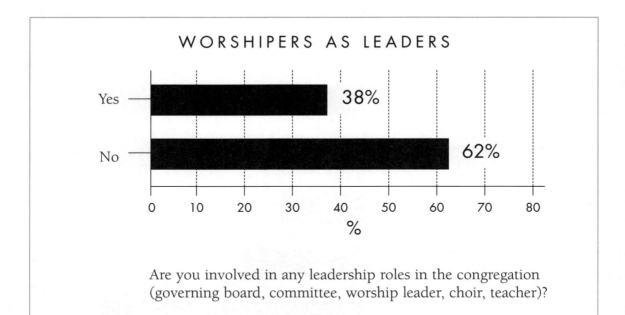

WORSHIPERS AS LEADERS

Are you involved in any leadership roles in the congregation (governing board, committee, worship leader, choir, teacher)?

Figure 4.2

Worshipers in Catholic parishes are less likely to get involved in decisions affecting parish life. But they are as likely as those in other faith groups to feel they have been given the opportunity to have a say in important decisions.

Participating—for how long? One-third of worshipers are new people who have been attending their current congregation for five years or less. (We'll look at new people in more depth later in this chapter and again in chapter 6.) Another third have been attending there for between 6 and 20 years, and 28% have been participating for more than 20 years. A small number (6%) are visitors to the congregation—including those who usually attend another congregation and those who don't usually attend services anywhere.

Participating—more or less? Only a small percentage (12%) of worshipers describe themselves as participating in congregational activities less than they did two years ago. A quarter (27%) boast they are participating more than they did in the past. The largest group (49%) depicts their participation as stable, not having changed much in the past two years.

Making financial contributions. Most congregations and parishes heavily depend on worshipers' monetary gifts in order to operate. Worshipers give to their congregations at quite diverse levels, and their level of giving is not associated with their income. In other words, people with large incomes do not necessarily give a higher percentage of their money than worshipers with more limited financial resources. The biblical understanding of tithing—giving 10% or more of earnings to the congregation—is practiced by fewer than one in five worshipers (19%). However, there is a wide gap in the practice of tithing between Catholics and other worshipers. While less than one in 10 Catholic worshipers tithe, almost one-third of Protestant worshipers are tithers. Catholics are more likely to say they give a small amount whenever they attend Mass (26%).

The more common giving practice among the majority of worshipers is to give a smaller percentage on a regular basis (27% give 5% to 9% of their income, and 27% give less than 5% of their income). Some (20%) give only a small amount whenever they attend worship services. A few (7%) never contribute money to the congregation. (See Figure 4.3.)

MYTH TRAP

Congregations grow by attracting new people who are not attending religious services anywhere.

A large percentage of new people who joined a congregation in the last five years transferred from another congregation of the same faith tradition (57%). Only 7% joined a congregation or parish for the first time. Those returning after not attending anywhere for some time were also a small percentage of all new people (18%). The remaining 18% of worshipers switched from a congregation of a different faith tradition. What new strategies might be required to attract people without a history of involvement in a faith community to your worship services and congregational activities?

It's All about Relationships

Many worshipers say their congregation or parish is like a family. Using phrases like "my church" or "our parish" connotes a sense of ownership and a close identification with the congregation. Many experts believe these horizontal connections are as important as the vertical connection with God for the congregation's ministry. In the next section, four subjective aspects of congregational relationships are explored—the sense of belonging, having friends in the congregation, the presence of conflict, and feelings about the key leader.

"I know I belong here." Congregations receive high marks for making people feel at home. Three out of four worshipers (79%) have a strong sense of belonging to their congregation. Almost half (46%) of all worshipers not only describe a strong sense of belonging but say this feeling has been growing. Protestants and those from other faith groups are more likely to say this sense of belonging is growing when compared to the experiences of Catholic worshipers.

"Some of my best friends go here." Two-thirds (67%) of all worshipers count at least some close friends among the other worshipers in their congregation; only a small percentage (14%) say *all* of their close friends attend there. A significant minority (16%) indicate that they have little contact with others from the congregation outside of scheduled activities, and 17% have some friends in their congregation but say their close friends don't attend there.

What about conflict? Like families, people in congregations do not always agree. How much conflict is there in congregations or, more accurately, how much are worshipers aware of disagreements? Half of the worshipers said that there had been no conflict in their congregation over the last two years. But one in five had noted "some conflict." Catholic worshipers reported slightly less conflict at this level than did Protestants or other faith groups. Only a small minority of worshipers (7%) mentioned major conflict. An even smaller number said that the conflict resulted in leaders or people leaving the congregation (4%).

Being a team. Do worshipers feel connected to the key leader in the congregation? Most worshipers (84%) agreed with the statement, "In general, there is a good match

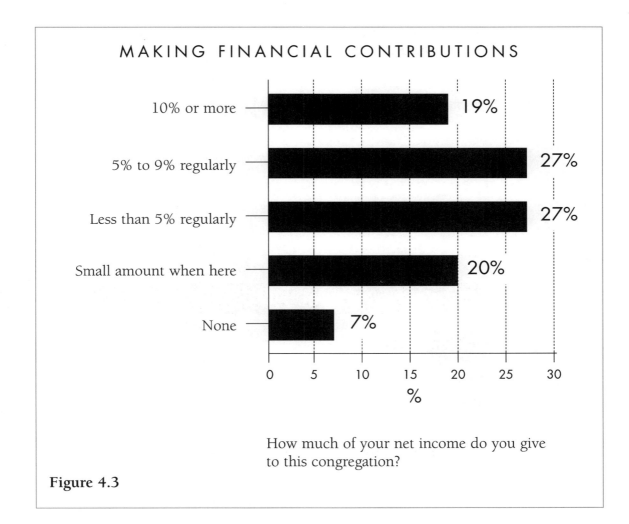

MAKING FINANCIAL CONTRIBUTIONS

10% or more — **19%**

5% to 9% regularly — **27%**

Less than 5% regularly — **27%**

Small amount when here — **20%**

None — **7%**

How much of your net income do you give to this congregation?

Figure 4.3

between our congregation and our minister, pastor, or priest." A very small number (only 3%) felt that their leader and congregation were not a good match, but some were neutral or unsure (12%). Unfortunately, a small number of unhappy people, especially if they hold leadership positions, can disrupt the harmony of congregation or parish life. (See Figure 4.4.)

Growing Congregations and Types of New People

Congregations with growing worship attendance fuel that growth in several ways. (See Figure 4.5.) New people (the 34% of all worshipers who have been attending

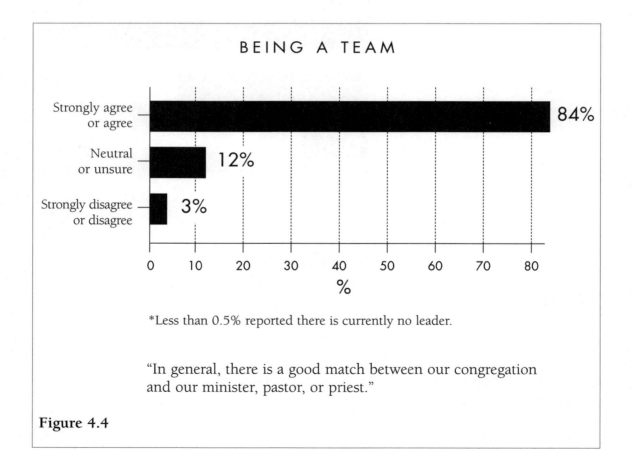

BEING A TEAM

Strongly agree or agree — 84%

Neutral or unsure — 12%

Strongly disagree or disagree — 3%

*Less than 0.5% reported there is currently no leader.

"In general, there is a good match between our congregation and our minister, pastor, or priest."

Figure 4.4

their current congregation for five years or less) come from four different faith backgrounds: *First-timers* (7% of all new people) are worshipers who have never regularly attended anywhere. *Returnees* (18% of worshipers attending five years or less) are those who at some point in their life participated in a community of faith and are now returning to worship services. For many returnees, this faith involvement took place when they were children and their parents took them to worship, Sunday or Sabbath school, or other religious activities. A period of absence from active participation is not unusual among worshipers, and this period of inactivity most often occurs during the twenties, with a return to religious activities prompted by marriage or the birth of children.

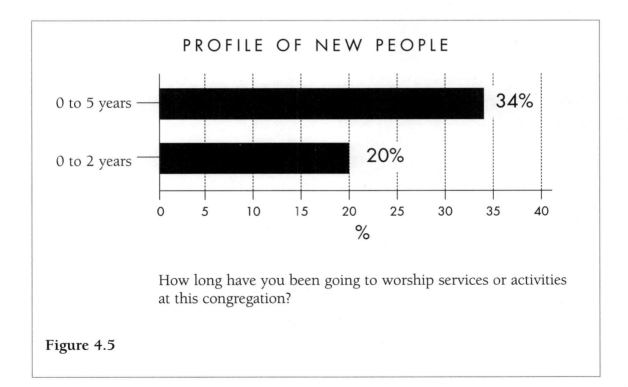

PROFILE OF NEW PEOPLE

How long have you been going to worship services or activities at this congregation?

Figure 4.5

Most of the growth in congregations comes from the other two types of new people—*switchers* and *transfers*. Switchers, who make up 18% of all new people, move or change from one type of faith community to another. Switching may be prompted by marriage to someone of a different faith background, moving to a new community, or changing values and preferences. Switching has become more common in the United States, with larger numbers of people engaging in "serial switching"—participation in three or more different faith communities during adulthood.

Switching among Protestant groups is more common than moving across the Protestant/Catholic divide or the Christian/non-Christian one. Only 9% of worshipers in Catholic parishes are switchers compared to almost three times that number (24%) among worshipers in Protestant churches and congregations of other faith traditions. Non-Catholic worshipers are also more likely to be returnees (22%) than Catholic worshipers (12%).

Transfers—religious participants who move their membership or participation from one congregation to another congregation of the same denomination or faith tradition—have also grown in number. Currently, transfers constitute 57% of new people in U.S. congregations. Greater social and geographic mobility means far fewer Americans stay in one place for a lifetime anymore. As they change jobs, schools, and dentists, and leave forwarding addresses, many search for a place of worship that is identical to the brand they left behind. While some people arrive in a new community and never find another worship site that meets their needs, or are too absorbed with new activities to search out a new worshiping community, many readily pick up their involvement in a congregation of the same denomination or faith tradition. That more than half of all new worshipers are transfers from other congregations indicates that many congregations are circulating regular attendees rather than enlarging the pool of people involved in communities of faith.

The gap between the faith background of new people worshiping in Catholic parishes and those in other congregations appears again when considering transfers. Three out of four new people in Catholic parishes have transferred from other Catholic parishes. Less than half (45%) of other worshipers, Protestants and those from other faith traditions, have transferred from a congregation of the same denomination or faith group. (See Figure 4.6.)

TYPES OF NEW PEOPLE*

	All Worshipers	Catholic Worshipers	Protestant and Other Worshipers
First-timers	7%	6%	9%
Returnees	18%	12%	22%
Switchers	18%	9%	24%
Transfers	57%	73%	45%

*New people are those attending the congregation for five years or less.

Figure 4.6

What Is There to Do Here?

What do congregations offer participants in addition to opportunities to worship? Many provide religious education, the chance to share with others in a small group, and the possibility of joining a prayer group.

Religious education. More than 90% of congregations offer a variety of religious education opportunities to worshipers. Almost all hold religious education classes, church school, or Sabbath school for children. In the average congregation with 90 in worship, about 15 children under the age of 12 take part in these classes. Almost 90% also offer similar classes for youth and for adults. About 10 youths between 12 and 18 years of age and 25 adults over the age of 18 participate in religious education in the average congregation.

Small groups. A majority of congregations (58%) offer small groups for sharing and spiritual growth, and half of those that do describe their small groups as an important part of their strategy to involve people in the congregation.

Group prayer life. Prayer groups meet in two-thirds of all congregations. They include a wide variety of types of groups, convened for many different purposes. (See Figure 4.7.)

TYPES OF PRAYER GROUPS

Prayer groups that meet infrequently 6%
Regular prayer groups that meet at certain times of the year 13%
Regular prayer groups that are part of a small-group program 21%
Regular prayer groups attached to specific classes, groups, or ministries 30%
Other types of prayer groups 35%
No organized prayer groups 32%

Figure 4.7

What Matters?

The majority of worshipers are attending services but participating in little or nothing else in their congregation. The thin layer of engagement in the total offerings of the congregation means that many worshipers miss out on a variety of opportunities available to them. The majority are not taking part in any small-group activity, serving as leaders, or involved in making congregational decisions. The majority are not major financial stakeholders, given their low levels of regular giving. Despite these behavioral patterns among worshipers, they *feel* connected to their parish or congregation. The average worshiper finds close friends in the community of faith, has a strong sense of belonging, and believes the leader is a good match for the needs of the congregation or parish.

What is the faith background of new people in the average congregation? The largest group among those attending for five years or less in Protestant churches, Catholic parishes, and other faith groups is transfers—those moving their membership or involvement from one congregation to another in the same denomination or faith group. The number of new people who are becoming involved in a faith community for the first time is quite small. Congregations are doing a far better job of attracting worshipers who have a history of parish or congregational association.

MARGARET BECAME THE FIRST PARISHIONER TO BE ASKED <u>NOT</u> TO WELCOME PEOPLE.

CHAPTER 5

OUTSIDE CONNECTIONS

Every species depends on its habitat to survive. Zoos spend considerable time and money researching what each inhabitant needs to thrive. Congregations likewise exist in time and space occupying a specific habitat. This chapter explores the relationships that worshipers have with their habitat—the local community of the congregation or parish. How do they make outside connections? Located in communities that are growing or declining, they welcome new people or say good-bye more times than they'd like. Some parishes are struggling to relate to large numbers of new people who speak a variety of languages. In some places, wheelchair-accessible ramps replace basketball hoops as the neighborhood changes from one teeming with young families to one full of empty-nest older couples. Congregations have a stake in their habitat indicated by their strong sense of place, a feeling of belonging to a particular piece of geography—their corner of the neighborhood, city, town, or county. How are congregations fed by their communities? Or more important, how do congregations and parishes feed, both spiritually and materially, their communities?

Some faith traditions make a clear distinction between two possible ways to relate to their context. One type of relating to the congregation's context is evangelism or efforts to bring new people into the faith community. Individual members and regular worshipers act to include outsiders in their faith community by inviting others and sharing their faith. A second avenue for relating to the community is through social service or advocacy efforts. Some see this second approach as another strategy for bringing new people into the congregation rather than a distinct ministry activity that may or may not result in new members. Both categories of relating to the community can be the result of individual efforts by worshipers or a collective strategy carried out by the congregation itself. Evangelism, or reaching out to nonmembers, is described below. Community service and advocacy efforts are described in the section that follows.

Reaching Out to Nonmembers

Inviting behavior. Less than half of worshipers (46%) invited someone—a friend or relative who is not currently attending a church, synagogue, or temple anywhere—to a worship service at their congregation in the last year. One in three say they are prepared to do so, but haven't in the last year. Worshipers in Catholic parishes are less likely to have issued such an invitation than are worshipers in other types of congregations. (See Figure 5.1.)

Talking the walk. Three out of four worshipers say they find it easy to talk about their faith, and some (16%) seek opportunities to do so. Others (12%) do not talk about their faith because they believe their life and actions are sufficient. (See Figure 5.2.)

Congregational efforts. In addition to the efforts of individual worshipers to invite others, most congregations and parishes collectively act to let others know of their

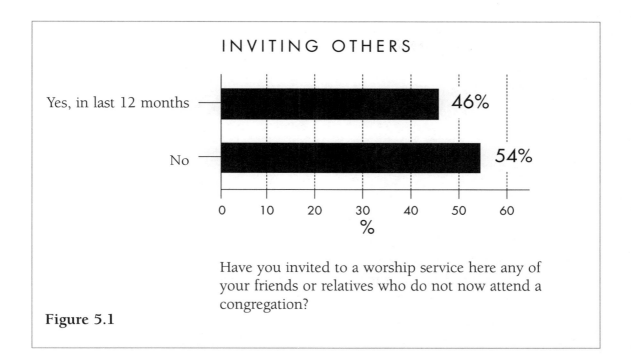

INVITING OTHERS

Yes, in last 12 months — 46%

No — 54%

Have you invited to a worship service here any of your friends or relatives who do not now attend a congregation?

Figure 5.1

TALKING ABOUT FAITH

Which of the following best describes your readiness to talk to others about your faith?

I do not have faith, so the question is not applicable 1%
I do not talk about my faith; my life and actions are sufficient 12%
I find it hard to talk about my faith in ordinary language 12%
I mostly feel at ease talking about my faith and do so if it comes up 59%
I feel at ease talking about my faith and seek opportunities to do so 16%

Figure 5.2

services and programs (such as placing an ad in the phone book or yellow pages). From a list of 14 such outreach activities (see Figure 5.3), congregations most often report encouraging their current worshipers to invite someone new to the congregation. Many also use mass mailings such as newsletters, letters, or flyers or mail letters or other information to people who have already visited the congregation or parish. On average, congregations report using six of these techniques.

CONGREGATIONAL OUTREACH ACTIVITIES

Encouraged people already in the congregation to invite a new person 90%

Sent a letter or material to people who visited your congregation 69%

Mailed or distributed newsletters, letters, or flyers 66%

Had an activity (e.g., fair, chili supper) to meet people in the neighborhood . . . 51%

Had someone from the congregation telephone people who
      visited your congregation 51%

Placed a paid ad in a newspaper or magazine 51%

Established or maintained a Web site for the congregation 43%

Had someone from the congregation go to the home of people who
      visited your congregation 42%

Placed a paid ad in the phone book or yellow pages 41%

Tried to identify and contact people who recently moved into the area 36%

Sponsored or participated in an outreach service or other
      public event intended to bring people into your congregation 35%

Advertised on radio or TV 25%

Had a special committee to work on recruiting new members 23%

Conducted or used a survey of the community 13%

Figure 5.3

Congregations also use other methods to include more people in their worship services, denomination, or faith tradition. Some (12%) have been involved in planting or growing a new congregation in the previous five years. A few have reorganized or started a new worship service either for a distinct age, racial or ethnic, socioeconomic, or interest group (7%). And others (9%) have reorganized or started a new worship service for people who do not normally attend (often called "seeker services").

Serving the Community

Most worshipers (79%) believe their congregation is strongly focused on serving the wider community. But is this in fact the case?

On my own—doing community service or advocacy. Many pastors describe their congregation as a group of worshipers who are highly involved in community service or advocacy work *not* connected to the local congregation. They believe that being part of a community of faith leads people to social service and social justice work. Is this the case? No. In fact, the majority of worshipers (69%) are *not* active in community service or advocacy work in the community apart from their congregation. If they are involved, they are five times more likely to be active in social service or charity groups (27%) than in advocacy, justice, or lobbying groups (5%). (See Figure 5.4.)

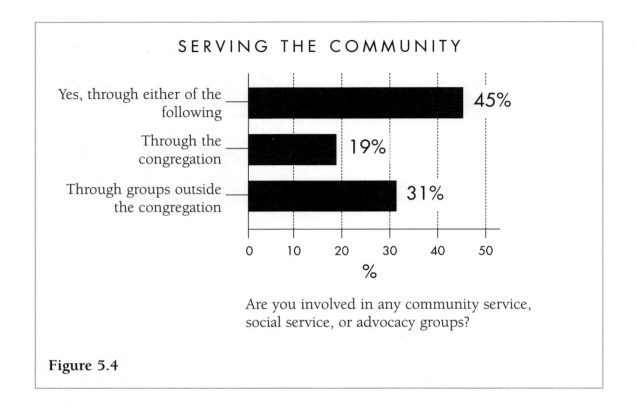

SERVING THE COMMUNITY

Yes, through either of the following — **45%**

Through the congregation — **19%**

Through groups outside the congregation — **31%**

0 10 20 30 40 50

%

Are you involved in any community service, social service, or advocacy groups?

Figure 5.4

Individual charity begins at home. Worshipers are often thought of as "good neighbors"—always giving and helpful to others. In fact, they are. In the 12 months before the survey, many prepared or gave food to someone outside their family or congregation (49%), loaned money to someone outside the family (30%), helped someone find a job (23%), and cared for someone outside their family who was very sick (22%). Some worshipers (73%) gave money to a charitable organization (other than the congregation) in the past year. (See Figure 5.5.)

Acts of advocacy and politics. Worshipers are more likely to vote than the average American. About three-quarters (76%) of worshipers say they voted in the last presidential election. Only about half of all Americans reported voting for president in November

2000.[1] In addition, worshipers are more involved in the political arena than the average American: In the last year, 21% worked with others to try to solve a community problem and 19% contacted an elected official about a public issue.[2] (See Figure 5.6.)

ACTS OF CHARITY

In the past 12 months, have you done any of the following? (Mark *all* that apply.)

Donated money to a charitable organization (other than this congregation) . . 73%
Donated or prepared food for someone outside your family or congregation . 49%
Loaned money to someone outside your family 30%
Helped someone outside your family find a job 23%
Cared for someone outside your family who was very sick 22%

Figure 5.5

ACTS OF ADVOCACY AND POLITICS

In the past 12 months, have you done any of the following? (Mark *all* that apply.)

Voted in the last presidential election 76%
Worked with others to try to solve a community problem 21%
Contacted an elected official about a public issue 19%

Figure 5.6

1. *Civic Engagement: Survey of Voters and Nonvoters* (Evanston, Ill.: Medill School of Journalism, Northwestern University, March 2001).

2. The General Social Survey (GSS) asked about both of these topics in a slightly different manner. GSS respondents were asked if they *ever* worked with others to try to solve a community problem, and 33% said yes. Among worshipers, 21% had done so *in the previous year.* GSS respondents were also asked if they had *ever* contacted or written to a representative or governmental official, and 27% said yes. Among worshipers, 19% had contacted an elected official *in the previous year*. The somewhat lower participation rates for worshipers are not surprising given that they were focusing on the previous year rather than a lifetime of possible political involvement. The General Social Survey, National Opinion Research Center at the University of Chicago.

Providing education. A few congregations provide an elementary school (7%). The average number of children enrolled in these schools is 210. Some congregations (2%) have junior high and/or high schools. The average number of students enrolled in these schools is 60.

Services offered through the congregation. We asked each congregation which of 23 services they have provided for people in the community or for their members in the last year (see Figure 5.7). The average congregation reported involvement in five areas. Only two were cited by a majority of congregations—emergency relief and counseling or support groups.

What Matters?

Congregations and parishes connect with their communities by welcoming new people and serving society's needs. Most congregations rely on informal, person-to-person contact to alert people in the community that they are welcome at worship services. Many also rely on print media (e.g., phone book, newspaper ads) to convey their message of welcome. Almost half have established a presence on the Internet as a way to connect to people in their community. But the majority of congregations take a low-tech approach to getting the word out about services and programs.

An individual approach surfaces again when characterizing the ways congregations relate to community needs. Most efforts are carried out by individual worshipers (e.g., voting, contacting elected officials, donating to charitable organizations). Acting collectively, congregations are most likely to help those in need through providing emergency relief in the form of food or clothes. Counseling or support groups are also offered by a majority of congregations. While these types of efforts are enormously important in any community, they tend not to address the ongoing systemic problems that may have given rise to the distress of individuals or families. Job training, community organizing, and housing programs, for example, are aimed at community social change and are less likely to be undertaken by congregations.

TYPES OF COMMUNITY SERVICE

Emergency relief or material assistance (food, clothes for the needy) 74%

Counseling or support groups (marriage or bereavement counseling, parenting groups, women's groups) 61%

Other social, recreational, or leisure activities 42%

Other programs for children and youth (job training, literacy program, scouting, sports) 31%

Health-related programs and activities (blood drives, screenings, health education) 29%

Other senior citizen programs or assistance (Meals on Wheels, transportation) . . 29%

Arts, music, or cultural activities or programs 28%

Day care, preschool, before- or after-school programs 25%

Prison or jail ministry 24%

Sporting activities or teams (intramural teams) 22%

Other welfare, community service, or social action activities not mentioned here 18%

Hobby or craft groups 16%

Voter registration or voter education 15%

Community-organizing or neighborhood-action groups 15%

Housing for other groups (crisis, youth shelters, homeless, students) 15%

Substance abuse or 12-step recovery programs 14%

Political or social justice activities (civil rights, human rights) 14%

Care for persons with disabilities (skills training, respite care, home care) 10%

Immigrant support activities (English as a second language, refugee support, interpreting service) 8%

Elementary school 8%

Housing for senior citizens (nursing homes, assisted living) 5%

Animal welfare or environmental activities 4%

Activities for unemployed people (preparation for job seeking, skills training) . . 3%

Figure 5.7

Nadine often thought of leaving, but didn't want to appear fickle.

CHAPTER 6

TYPES OF WORSHIPERS

A field guide promises a comprehensive profile of all the specific "subspecies" in a general category. For example, did you know there are 52 different breeds of cows? Subspecies are simply subcategories or subdivisions of a general category. In this chapter, the field guide describes some of the many types of worshipers—frequent attendees and new people—and their unique field marks. The worshiper subspecies are arranged in order from the most common—the frequent worshiper who attends services every week—to the more rare or exotic—someone visiting a congregation for the first time.

The 83%: Weekly Worshipers

The most common worshiper is someone who reports attending every week.[1] Surprisingly, this group makes up 83% of all worshipers. Are they different in any way from the less frequent worshiper—the 17% who attend services occasionally?

---

1. Because the survey was given in worship, the more frequent attendees are more likely to have been present on the day it was given. For example, someone who attends worship services every week is sure to have been there no matter which week the survey was given. Someone who attends only once a month would be far less likely to have been in worship on that day.

Denomination or faith group. Worshipers in Catholic parishes are more likely to be frequent attendees than worshipers from other faith groups. While 88% of Catholic worshipers attend weekly, only 78% of Protestants and other faith groups attend weekly. Catholicism emphasizes the importance of attending Mass, and this expectation yields more frequent attendance among Catholics.

Long-term attendance. Long-term commitment to the congregation yields higher rates of worship attendance. Weekly worshipers are twice as likely to be found among those who have been attending the congregation for 20 years or more. Those who have been attending two years or less are half as likely to attend *less* frequently than once a week.

Involvement in other activities. Those who attend worship week after week are twice as likely as occasional worshipers to be involved in congregational small groups (such as church or Sabbath school; prayer, discussion, or Bible study groups; or social or fellowship groups) and other congregational activities (such as evangelism or community service). They are also twice as likely to hold a leadership position in the parish or congregation.

Big givers. Worshipers who attend weekly are three times as likely as other worshipers to give 10% or more of their income to the congregation (21% compared to just 7%). Weekly worshipers are twice as likely to give 5% or more of their income (30% compared to 15%). Clearly, regular attendance fosters greater financial support for the congregation. A large percentage of occasional attendees (40%) report they give a small amount whenever they are in services.

Gender. While more women sit in the pews, there is barely a gender difference in how frequently people attend services. Women are only slightly more likely to attend worship on a weekly basis than men. Sixty-two percent of all frequent worshipers are women; 59% of less frequent worshipers are women.

Age. People 65 years of age and older attend services more frequently than the average worshiper. Younger adults, between 25 and 44 years of age, attend religious services less frequently than worshipers in other age groups.

Work. Frequent worshipers are more likely to be retired than those who attend less often. Occasional worshipers are more likely to report full- or part-time employment.

Education and income. Surprisingly, looking at education and household income won't help you identify frequent worshipers. Weekly attendees are neither more educated nor less educated than those who attend less often. Additionally, annual income is not related to the frequency of attendance of worshipers.

Race, ethnicity, and nationality. Whites are slightly more likely to be weekly attendees than black or Hispanic attendees. There are no differences in attendance by racial category for Asian, Indian, or other racial or ethnic worshipers. Weekly worshipers are more likely to have been born in the United States. Current residents born outside the United States in non-English-speaking countries are less frequent in their attendance than other worshipers.

Marital status. Married people, especially those in their first marriages, are more likely to go to religious services on a weekly basis. Those who have never been married are less frequent in their worship attendance. Widowed people are also overrepresented among the weekly worshipers, being almost twice as likely to be present as other types of singles.

Children. People with children residing at home were less frequent in their attendance than those with no children at home.

Travel time. It's not living closer that gets weekly worshipers there more often. Frequent attendees spend the same amount of time traveling to worship as those who come less often. (See Figure 6.1.)

THE 83%—WEEKLY WORSHIPERS: A PROFILE

Attending 20 years or more 30%

Involved in a small group 60%

Gives 10% or more 21%

Women 62%

65 years of age or older 26%

Retired 27%

Married 67%

No children residing at home 41%

Figure 6.1

The 34%: New People

As mentioned in chapter 4, worshipers can be divided into three approximately equal-sized groups. About one in three are new people, worshipers attending services at their current congregation five years or less. Another third have been attending services there between 6 and 20 years. And a final third (28%) have been attending more than 20 years. (About 6% are visitors from another congregation or people who don't regularly attend anywhere else.) The proportion of new people attending worship services suggests a fairly high turnover rate in the average faith community. What are the field marks of worshipers who have been attending for five years or less?

Denomination or faith group. More worshipers in Protestant churches and congregations of other faith groups are found among the pool of new people in the congregation than in Catholic parishes.

Low levels of involvement. New people are less involved in small groups of all types (49% of new people compared to 55% for all worshipers). The biggest gap in their small-group involvement compared to other worshipers is in their participation in congregational social or fellowship groups (21% participate compared to 27% for all worshipers). Even more significant is their lower rate of leadership roles in the congregation. This finding suggests that the entrance ramps to congregational involvement at a leadership level are long and narrow.

The pattern of less involvement in congregational activities appears in a third way. New people are less likely to take part in activities of the congregation or parish that involve outreach, evangelism, community service, or advocacy.

Giving. The giving patterns of new people are a mixed picture. New people are just as likely as long-term participants to give 10% or more of their income to the congregation. However, new worshipers report lower levels of regular giving (between 5% and 9%) when compared to long-term worshipers. They are more likely to give just small amounts of money whenever they attend services.

Age. New people are younger than the average worshiper by eight years. The largest percentage of new worshipers (45%) are in the 25-to-44-year-old group. Less than one-third of all worshipers fall in the same age bracket.

Work. Working full- or part-time is more common among the newer worshipers. In fact, two out of three new people are employed. This finding is clearly related to the lower average age of these worshipers.

Education. Even more educated than the average worshiper, many new people hold college degrees or more advanced degrees (40%), and a large group have attained a high school diploma or more education (88%).

Marital status and children. New people are less likely than long-term participants to be in their first marriage. They are more likely than longtime worshipers to have never married or to be remarried after divorce. Again, these patterns are probably associated with the average age of new worshipers.

Nondistinguishing field marks. While new people look different from long-term worshipers in some ways, in other ways they are quite similar. New people are similar to typical worshipers in terms of gender, income, race and ethnicity, and place of birth. (See Figure 6.2.)

First-Time Worship Visitors

Every congregation invites and welcomes new people to attend. Yet across worship services in more than 2,000 American congregations, only 2% of those attending were present in that congregation for the first time. Who are these rare worshipers? What are their field marks?

THE 34%—NEW PEOPLE*: A PROFILE

Involved in a small group	49%
Gives 10% or more	18%
Women	60%
25 to 44 years of age	45%
Employed full- or part-time	65%
College or more advanced degree	40%
Married	62%
No children residing at home	36%

*New people are those attending for five years or less.

Figure 6.2

Denomination or faith group. Catholic parishes were as likely to have first-time visitors attending their Masses as Protestant churches or congregations of other faith groups (e.g., Jews). Slightly more than half (52%) of these first-time worshipers were attending Mass at a new parish; the remainder (48%) were attending services in a Protestant congregation or place of worship for another faith group.

History of worship attendance. The majority of first-time visitors (67%) reported they had been participating in another congregation before coming to worship in one of the study's congregations. But 13% said they had never regularly attended anywhere before visiting the congregation. Another 15% said that prior to visiting this congregation they had not been attending anywhere for several years.

Age. The largest group of first-time worship visitors (39%) consists of people between the ages of 25 and 44. The average age of these rare worshipers is 41, fully 9 years younger than the average worshiper.

Gender. More first-time worship visitors are women than men (59% compared to 41%), a gender ratio almost identical to all worshipers.

Work. Visitors look quite similar to all worshipers in terms of their employment profile. Most (57%) are working full- or part-time. However, more students and fewer retired people are found among the first-time visitors than in the general worshiper population.

Marital status. While only one-third of all worshipers are not married, a larger portion (46%) of all first-time worship visitors are not married. More than one in four (27%) of these visitors have never been married; 10% are divorced or separated; 5% are living in a committed relationship but are not married; and 4% are widowed. (See Figure 6.3.)

What Matters?

Why identify types of worshipers? The answer goes to the heart of the congregation's purpose: What are we trying to do here? What is God calling us to do and be as a congregation? People sitting in the pews may look like average Americans to the uninformed observer. However, this chapter observes not only that worshipers are far from typical

THE 2% — FIRST-TIME VISITORS: A PROFILE

Married 54%

Women 59%

Employed full- or part-time 57%

25 to 44 years of age 39%

Attending elsewhere recently 67%

Returning after long-term absence 15%

Never regularly attended anywhere 13%

Figure 6.3

COMPARING WORSHIPERS

	All Worshipers	Worshipers in Catholic Parishes	Worshipers in Protestant and Other Congregations
Weekly worshipers	83%	88%	78%
New people	34%	32%	39%
First-time visitors	2%	2%	3%

Figure 6.4

Americans but that worshipers differ from one another in important ways. It is easy to make assumptions about why people come, what types of people are going to be most committed, and what must be done to "fix" what we think doesn't work. Programs, strategies, planning, and all sorts of efforts can be made that yield little in terms of furthering the congregation's mission. (See Figure 6.4.)

Like bird-watching, not too much gear is needed to spot types of worshipers. Look for clues in terms of the factors discussed in this chapter and ask: What kind are they? Knowing "who comes to worship services" is the first step in thinking about "why people come." To better understand "why they come," review the field marks of weekly worshipers, new people, and first-time visitors. Who are congregations currently attracting and welcoming to their worship services and congregational activities? Why is this the case?

The field marks of worshipers laid out in this chapter are meant to assist leaders in seeing their congregation in bold relief. What are the characteristics that make your congregation stand out? Use these as clues to lead you as you seek to answer the most important question: "What are we trying to do here?"

CHAPTER 7

IDENTITY, LEADERSHIP, VISION

This final chapter illustrates the most difficult and yet most important part of any guided exploration: Where are we headed? What is our sense of direction? Where do we think we're going? Any guide can be of only limited use if we have little idea about our future destination. What is our goal and in which direction should we take our first step?

Congregations, like people, live in the present. But they have a story about their past that gives meaning to today. Likewise, they have a mental map about what the future looks like. Is the future more of the same or does it look radically different? The last contribution of this guide is to explore three interrelated themes: identity—who we think we are; leadership—what the role of our leaders is in helping us to understand present realities and to create a positive future; and vision—what the depth and breadth of our future mission are.

Identity: Who Do We Think We Are?

We are what we value. What do worshipers most value about their congregations? What worshipers value is the best gauge of their identity. It's difficult to name just one favorite, so we asked worshipers to choose up to three aspects of their congregation that they particularly value. Great diversity of opinion about the most treasured aspects of congregational life emerged. Almost half (49%) chose sharing the sacrament of Holy Communion (i.e., sharing in the Eucharist, the Lord's Supper). The second most-valued feature is the sermons, preaching, or homilies. Finally, one-third value the traditional style of worship or music characteristic of their congregation. Other areas of congregational life were chosen by smaller numbers of people. Only 16% chose each of the following aspects as their most valued: reaching the unchurched and ministry for children and youth. (See Figure 7.1.)

Leadership: Can You Help Us Get There from Here?

Perceptions about the roles of the pastor.[1] People in the pew believe their minister, pastor, or priest carries out the following roles: conducting worship (61%), teaching people about the faith (58%), visiting or counseling people (36%), offering prayer or being a spiritual role model (26%), providing a vision and goals for the future (24%), administering the work of the congregation (18%), training people for ministry and mission (16%), converting others to the faith (13%), and confronting social injustices (11%). Worshipers could mark up to three of these roles. (See Figure 7.2.)

Leadership style of pastor. Almost half of attendees portray the leadership style of the minister, pastor, or priest as one that inspires people to take action. Others (20%) describe their leader's style as one "that tends to take charge." A reactive style, "leader-

---

1. Worshipers in Catholic parishes were not asked this question on the surveys distributed during Mass. A question relevant to the Catholic parish life was substituted. Only worshipers in Protestant churches and congregations of other faith traditions responded to this item.

WE ARE WHAT WE VALUE

Which of the following aspects of this congregation do you personally most value? (Mark up to *three* options.)

Sharing in Holy Communion, Eucharist, or the Lord's Supper	49%
Sermons, preaching, or homilies	40%
Traditional style of worship or music	32%
Contemporary style of worship or music	17%
Ministry for children or youth	16%
Reaching those who do not attend church	16%
Wider community care or social justice emphasis	15%
Bible study or prayer groups, other discussion groups	14%
Social activities or meeting new people	13%
Practical care for one another in times of need	13%
Openness to social diversity	10%
Prayer ministry for one another	9%
The congregation's school or preschool	8%
Adult church-school or Sabbath-school class	6%

Figure 7.1

ship that acts on goals that people here have been involved in setting," is less likely to be reported by worshipers (only 15%). And even fewer (4%) say "the people start most things" in their congregation. (See Figure 7.3.)

Ministers take into account worshipers' ideas. In general worshipers say their minister, pastor, or priest takes into account the ideas of those who worship in the congregation to "a great extent" (44%) or to "some extent" (28%). Some "don't know"

PERCEPTIONS ABOUT THE ROLES OF THE PASTOR

What do you think are the main roles that your minister, pastor, or priest actually carries out here? (Mark up to *three* options.)

Conducting worship or administering the sacraments 61%
Teaching people about the faith 58%
Visiting, counseling, and helping people 36%
Offering prayer or being a spiritual role model 26%
Providing a vision and goals for the future 24%
Administering the work of the congregation 18%
Training people for ministry and mission 16%
Converting others to the faith 13%
Confronting social injustices 11%
Don't know 5%

*This question was not asked of worshipers in Catholic parishes.

Figure 7.2

LEADERSHIP STYLE OF PASTOR

Leadership that tends to take charge 20%
Leadership that inspires people to take action 46%
Leadership that acts on goals that people here have been involved in setting . . . 15%
Leadership where the people start most things 4%
There is currently no leader here 1%
Don't know 15%

Figure 7.3

(22%) whether the minister is open to others' ideas. Only 6% describe their leader as someone who doesn't take into account the ideas of worshipers.

Another good sign. The majority (74%) report their congregation's leaders have encouraged them to find and use their gifts and skills in the congregation or parish. But one in four worshipers say this encouragement has not happened at all or "don't know" if it has or not.

Being a team. Eight out of ten worshipers (84%) see their minister, pastor, or priest as a good match for the congregation. Only 3% are clearly not satisfied with the current leadership in the congregation. Twelve percent are unsure about the fit between the congregation and the current leader.

A Vision for the Future

Possibilities for the future. Do worshipers believe their congregation has a clear vision, goals, or direction for its ministry and mission? More than two out of three (71%) say "yes" and most (59%) are committed to the congregation's direction. But one in three worshipers (29%) characterize their congregation as not having a vision or as having ideas but no clear goals or direction. (See Figure 7.4.)

Excitement about the future. Most of those attending worship (80%) are excited about their congregation's future. Some are neutral (18%), but only a few are not excited (2%).

> # GUIDELINES
>
> **Worshipers say what they most value in their congregation is sharing the sacrament of Holy Communion, the sermons or homilies, and traditional worship and music.**
>
> *What do these values express about the purpose of the congregation or parish? Is there a disconnection between what we value and the spiritual needs of the community? Are the values of the congregation consistent with its planned future directions? How do the congregation's values challenge worshipers to live their faith in the world? What one or two steps could our parish or congregation take to improve the consistency between what we value and what we do?*

POSSIBILITIES FOR THE FUTURE

Does this congregation have a clear vision, goals, or direction for its ministry and mission?

I am not aware of such a vision, goals, or direction 19%

There are ideas but no clear vision, goals, or direction 10%

Yes, and I am strongly committed to them 31%

Yes, and I am partly committed to them 28%

Yes, but I am not committed to them 12%

Figure 7.4

Another indicator of hopefulness about the future. The largest percentage of worshipers (34%) assert that their congregation is moving in new directions. Another one in five picture their congregation as currently deciding on new directions. But one in ten report their congregation is faithfully maintaining past directions. A small minority (5%) feel the congregation needs to get back to the way things were done in the past. (See Figure 7.5.)

Is the congregation ready to try something new? The potential for change exists in most congregations: 61% of all worshipers believe their congregation is always ready to try something new. Yet 30% are unsure if their congregation is ready to change, and 9% say their congregation is not ready for change.

Worshipers see their leaders as primarily conducting worship and teaching people about the faith. While these are essential roles in a community of faith, few report that one of their leader's primary roles is helping their congregation to form and implement a vision for the future. Leaders are described as inspiring others, as taking their ideas into account, and as a good fit with the needs of their congregation. Worshipers describe themselves as open to change and positive about their congregation's future. These findings suggest somewhat of a disconnection between the openness of worshipers to change and new directions and the priorities of their leaders.

Who Speaks for Congregations?

Reality matters, and what people do with facts matters even more. This field guide asserts that congregations and their leaders can reach data-driven decisions that make a difference. Worshipers across America have now told their story about what matters to them. They join the long tradition of people of faith who have always told stories that help them honor the past and give definition to the future. Some stories grow larger and more significant with time because they recount how we survived and came to be the people of God. An example of such a story illustrates the importance once again of using accurate information. Noah, a righteous man, built a cypress wood ark. He used correct information—precise measurements of length, width, and height—to create the boat that would carry people and animals to a new day in a new world. Just as essential as building a bridge that won't collapse, he assembled a boat that wouldn't sink. Acting on accurate information as a person of faith, he became a part of the larger story of creation becoming new creation.

But isn't using facts inconsistent with acting out of faith? Does faith matter? Acting on faith is not the same as acting out of ignorance. And choosing to include accurate information as part of the equation when making congregational decisions does not exclude acting on faith. In the New Testament, Christ tells Peter, an expert fisherman, to drop his net into the water. Peter knows that the water contains no fish. When by faith he follows the directive anyway, his bulging net comes out of the water so full of fish that it breaks from the weight. In another story about vast numbers, Jesus directs his disciples to take a young boy's lunch and share it with 5,000 people. The singular, simple meal feeds the entire crowd, with plenty to spare. From the Old Testament comes another favorite numbers story. David, a shepherd boy, gathered a mere five stones. So armed, he slew a giant named Goliath.

God calls congregations to such faith-filled actions. They calculate the risks; gather their stones, bread, or nets; and move ahead in faith. Compelled by their calling as a congregation, worshipers find their directive so clear it defines who they are, why they exist, and what they can do. Faith moves mountains, feeds people spiritually, overcomes obstacles, and makes use of available resources. May your congregation go and do likewise.

U.S. Congregational Life Survey Methodology

Over 300,000 worshipers in over 2,000 congregations across America participated in the U.S. Congregational Life Survey, making it the largest survey of worshipers in America ever conducted. Three types of surveys were completed in each participating congregation: (1) an attendee survey completed by all worshipers age 15 and older who attended worship services during the weekend of April 29, 2001; (2) a congregational profile describing the congregation's facilities, staff, programs, and worship services completed by one person in the congregation; and (3) a leader survey completed by the pastor, priest, minister, rabbi, or other leader. Together the information collected provides a unique three-dimensional look at religious life in America.

The National Opinion Research Center (NORC) at the University of Chicago identified a random sample of U.S. congregations attended by individuals who participated in the General Social Survey (GSS) in the year 2000. All GSS participants who reported that they attended worship at least once in the prior year were asked to name the place where they worshiped. Since the GSS involves a national random sample of individuals, congregations identified by GSS participants comprise a national random sample of congregations. NORC researchers verified that each nominated congregation was an actual congregation and then invited each congregation to participate in the project. Of 1,214 nominated and verified congregations, 807 agreed to participate (66%), and 434 returned completed surveys from their worshipers (36%). (A wide variety of reasons were given by congregations that chose not to participate.) Worshipers in these congregations, representing all 50 states, completed 122,043 attendee surveys, which are the primary source of the findings reported here. The size of this scientific statistical sample far exceeds the size of most national surveys. Studies designed to provide a representative profile of adults living in the United States typically include about 1,000 people.

Denominations were also invited and encouraged to draw a random sample of their congregations. Denominational samples were large enough so that the results are representative of worshipers and congregations in each denomination. This allows denominations to compare their "typical" congregation and worshiper to congregations and worshipers in other denominations. Denominations participating in this oversampling procedure were Church of the Nazarene, Evangelical Lutheran Church in America (ELCA), Presbyterian Church (U.S.A.), Roman Catholic Church, Seventh-day Adventist Church, Southern Baptist Convention, United Methodist Church (UMC), and United Church of Christ (UCC). Results from these oversamples are not included here.

Additional information about the methods used in this study are available on our Web site: www.uscongregations.org. Congregations interested in comparing their worshipers to these national benchmarks can contact U.S. Congregations to order materials. Call 1-888-728-7228, ex. 2040 or visit their Web site at www.uscongregations.org.

PARTICIPATING CONGREGATIONS

The U.S. Congregational Life Survey included congregations from all of the following denominations and faith groups:

African Methodist Episcopal Church
African Methodist Episcopal Zion Church
American Baptist Churches in the U.S.A.
Assemblies of God, General Council of
Baptist (unspecified)
Bible Way Church, Worldwide
Buddhist Communities
Christian Reformed Church in North America
Christian and Missionary Alliances, The
Christian Church (Disciples of Christ)
Church of God
Church of the Nazarene
Church of Jesus Christ of Latter-day Saints, The

Church of God (Anderson, Indiana)
Church of God in Christ
Churches of Christ
Conservation Baptist Association of America
Conservative Judaism
Episcopal Church, The
Episcopal/Anglican
Evangelical Lutheran Church in America
Foursquare Gospel, International Church of the
Free Methodist Church of North America
Free Will Baptist
Free Lutheran Congregation, The Association of

General Association of Regular Baptist
  Church
Greek Orthodox Archdiocese of North
  and South America
Lutheran Church, the Missouri Synod
Lutheran (unspecified)
Mennonite (unspecified)
Mennonite Church
Missionary
National Baptist Convention, U.S.A., Inc.
Nondenominational congregations
Pentecostal (unspecified)
Presbyterian (unspecified)
Presbyterian Church (U.S.A.)

Presbyterian Church in America, The
Reorganized Church of Jesus Christ of
  Latter-day Saints
Reform Judaism
Roman Catholic Church
Seventh-day Adventist Church
Southern Baptist Convention
Unitarian Universalist Association
United Methodist Church, The
United Baptist
United Church of Christ
United Pentecostal Church, International
Unity of the Brethren
Wesleyan Church, The

GLOSSARY

Average, mean, median: A mean and a median are two ways to estimate the average of a set of numbers. Median refers to the middle number in an ordered series. For example, the median age for a group of people aged 12, 21, 28, 35, and 64 years would be 28 years—the middle score in the series. Mean refers to the mathematical average of values in a series; in the example, the mean age would be calculated by adding all the scores and dividing by the number of scores, as: (12+21+28+35+64)/5, or 32 years.

Congregation: A congregation is an assembly of people gathered for the purpose of religious worship or teachings. Congregations are voluntary organizations of individuals who join together as a religious community. A *church* is one type of congregation, but congregations also include synagogues, temples, and mosques.

Congregational profile: Each participating congregation completed a congregational profile that provided factual information about the congregation—its size, programs, staff, and finances.

Denomination: A specific, organized religious body. Many congregations are affiliated with a denomination or other association of congregations, but some are not. Appendix 2 shows the denominations with which participating congregations are affiliated.

First-timers: First-timers are new people (attending the congregation for five years or less) who have never participated in a congregation before their current congregation.

Leader: The leader survey was completed by one key leader in each congregation. This was usually the senior or solo pastor or minister, a co-pastor, an interim pastor, a priest, or rabbi. In some congregations, the primary leader is not a minister, but rather a lay leader. The leader survey gathered information about the background and ministry experiences of congregational leaders.

Long-term attendees: Long-term attendees are those who have been participating in the particular congregation for more than five years.

National average: The national average summarizes the answers given by all worshipers who completed the survey. It allows each participating congregation to compare their worshipers' answers to the answers of all worshipers.

New people: Worshipers or attendees who have been coming to the particular congregation for five years or less. There are four types of new people: first-timers, returnees, switchers, and transfers.

Random sample: A random sample is a subset of an entire population in which each element of the population has an equal chance of being selected. Results from a random sample can be generalized to the entire population. The U.S. Congregational Life Survey was completed by a random sample of congregations in the United States, and thus, the results of the survey are representative of worshipers and congregations across the country.

Returnees: Returnees are new people (attending the congregation for five years or less) who had participated in a congregation previously (perhaps when growing up), but who had not been involved in a congregation immediately prior to coming to their current congregation.

Switchers: Switchers are new people (attending the congregation for five years or less) who have switched denominations or faith groups when they began coming to their current congregation. Someone who leaves a Catholic church and begins attending a Lutheran church or someone who leaves a Baptist church to attend a Unitarian congregation would be a switcher.

Transfers: Transfers are new people (attending the congregation for five years or less) who were attending another congregation of the same denomination or faith group before coming to this particular congregation. Someone who leaves one Episcopal church and begins attending another Episcopal church would be a transfer.

Visitors: Visitors are attendees who are not regular participants in the congregation. Visitors include those who are beginning to look for a new worship community, those who might be attending because they were invited by a current attendee, and those visiting from out of town.

Worshipers or attendees: Worshipers or attendees are people who participate in worship—whether they are members of the congregation or not. Worshipers include members, people in the process of joining, visitors, and those who regularly participate in the congregation's activities but for whatever reason are not members. (For example, some denominations or faith groups do not allow ordained clergy to join a particular congregation.) All attendees 15 years of age and up were invited to take part in the survey.

Worship services: The U.S. Congregational Life Survey was completed during all regularly scheduled worship services of participating congregations.